Exploring Central London

LONDON
VISITOR & CONVENTION BUREAU
Welcome

£1·95

ABOUT THE LVCB

The London Visitor and Convention Bureau is the official tourist board for Greater London. It was established in 1963 as the London Tourist Board and changed its name in 1985 to the London Visitor and Convention Bureau. It promotes London in Britain and overseas in cooperation with the British Tourist Authority; it operates its own tourist information centres and assists local authorities in their tourist promotion and information services. See list of tourist information centres in Greater London on the back cover.

The London Visitor and Convention Bureau is at 26 Grosvenor Gardens, London SW1W 0DU (written enquiries only). Tourist Information Service Telephone: 01-730 3488.

Research: Christina O'Neill
Series Editor: Ylva French.
Production Editor: Helen Cameron.
Design and Production: Blyth-Lee Associates.
ISBN 0 946837 04 X
© London Tourist Board Ltd., 1986.

The information in this booklet was believed to be correct at the time of going to print. Opening times quoted are for 1986. LVCB cannot accept any responsibility for any errors or omissions.

CONTENTS

This is a borough by borough guide to central London, from west to east. Please refer to map on inside back cover.

	Page
ABOUT LVCB	Inside Front Cover
INTRODUCTION	2
PRACTICAL TIPS	2
GETTING AROUND LONDON	4
TRAVEL INFORMATION	6
KENSINGTON & CHELSEA	7
WESTMINSTER	14
THEATRE LIST	26
LAMBETH	29
CAMDEN	32
CITY	38
ISLINGTON	47
TOWER HAMLETS	51
SOUTHWARK	56
SUBJECT INDEX	59
INDEX	61
PUBLICATIONS	64
MAP	Inside Back Cover
TOURIST INFORMATION CENTRES	Back Page

KEY

- ⊖ Nearest London Transport Underground Station
- ⇌ Nearest British Rail Station
- ♿ Access for disabled visitors
- (L) Member of the LVCB

INTRODUCTION

This is a new guide to Central London researched and written by staff at the London Visitor and Convention Bureau, London's official tourist board. It is the companion volume to LVCB's *Exploring Outer London* guide and uses the same borough by borough approach.

In this guide you will find all of London's major attractions, plus some more unusual ones, listed under each borough, within the Central area as indicated on the map (see inside cover). In some cases attractions on the fringes of the central area such as Clerkenwell, Southwark and parts of the south bank have been covered in both the Central and Outer London guides.

Many visitors to London and quite a few Londoners will have little idea of which borough a particular attraction is in. Please use the general index at the back of the book. We have also included a subject index for those who wish to explore particular subjects such as art, famous people, military history, and so on.

Places of interest are closed on Christmas Day and usually on Boxing Day, New Year's Day, Good Friday and the May Bank Holiday (first Monday in May). Check opening times, if in doubt. Disabled access has been indicated but is based on each attraction's own assessment; check if in doubt. Groups should book in advance at smaller museums and galleries; educational visits, tours and lectures can be arranged at most museums and galleries.

A Greater London map on the inside back cover, shows the individual London boroughs. A good map is essential for exploring London; see list of publications on p. 64.

A few tips: ★ *Don't try to do too much* in one day ★ *do ask Londoners the way,* but don't expect too much when they are rushing to and from work – they will be friendlier in the pub at the end of the day ★ London is a safe and secure city but as in any other major city *watch your wallet and handbag* in crowded places, particularly pubs, winebars, shops, markets, on public transport and in cinemas ★ London is a multi-racial city with a cosmopolitan population from many parts of the world; take advantage of the benefits this brings in terms of cultural experiences and choice of ethnic foods ★ London's local councils do their best to keep the streets clean, *please support them by not dropping your litter* ★ London's public transport system closes down between midnight and 0600, *use a night-bus from Trafalgar Square, or a black cab* ★ if you use an *unlicensed mini-cab, make sure you have agreed the fare* beforehand ★ *check commission charges and exchange rates* at banks and bureaux de change.

Make the most of London and don't hesitate to use our tourist information services. *The Editor.*

GETTING AROUND LONDON

Travelling around Central London is generally quick and easy by public transport. The underground system serves most parts of the capital and for outer London there are convenient British Rail suburban services. (See *Exploring Outer London* p. 64).

The bus network is extensive and a trip on a double decker bus can be a sightseeing tour in itself. Single decker buses operate on certain routes, such as between railway stations, and on those you pay the driver as you enter or put your money in a slot. On most double decker buses the conductor will collect the fare.

The transport system extends to London's two major airports. Heathrow is served by underground and by special Air Buses and Green Line coach services. Gatwick is served by high-speed rail services into Victoria Station.

It is well worth while buying a special travel discount ticket not only to save money but to save time at ticket offices.

Special discount tickets
The *London Explorer* ticket is available for 1, 3, 4 and 7 days offering unlimited travel on the red London buses and underground train network as well as discount vouchers for many places of interest, including the London Transport Museum, the Guinness World of Records, Madame Tussauds and London Zoo.

The *Capital Card* combines rail, underground, and bus travel for a minimum of 1 week. A one-day, off peak card is also available from London Regional Transport and British Rail ticket offices.

The *One Day Travel Card,* and the *Travel Card* season ticket valid for a minimum of 1 week (for which a passport sized photograph is required) give unlimited travel on the bus and underground network within one of a choice of five zones.

These tickets are available from London Regional Transport ticket offices.

Children of 14 and 15 years require a child rate photo card to use when purchasing and using any special discount tickets as well as the normal single and return tickets at the child rate. These are available from post offices and you need two passport photographs and proof of age (birth certificate, passport or medical card).

Travelling in the Rush Hour
London's underground and buses are very busy during the morning rush hour from 0800 to 0930 approximately and from 1600 to 1800. The roads in the suburban areas tend to be particularly congested at these times as well, whereas central London can be congested throughout the day.

Sightseeing by car in centr
those who are not familia
Parking is difficult and e
those parked illegally is ef
as well as British registere

Sightseeing by black cab
or in a chauffeur driven ca........................ to
coach trips, (see p.6) and need not be expensive if several
are sharing. Black cabs are also an efficient and quick way
of getting around central London. They can be hailed or
booked in advance by phoning one of the following: Dial a
Cab 01-253 5000; Radio Taxi Cabs 01-272 0272.

River and Canal trips
The River Thames once at the heart of London's commercial
life has been superseded as a highway by roads, the
underground and railways. But there are regular tours by
riverboats which operate from Westminster, Charing Cross
and Tower Piers; also Festival Pier on the South Bank in the
summer. Through the year there are frequent departures to
the Tower and Greenwich as well as the Thames Barrier (see
Exploring Outer London). In the summer months and during
weekends in the spring and autumn riverboats also go
upstream from Westminster Pier to Kew and Hampton
Court. (Check with LVCB's riverboat information service on
01-730 4812).

London's canal network was established as part of the
industrial revolution. In recent years the canals have been
reclaimed for leisure and the footpaths opened for walkers.
Several waterbuses operate regularly along the Regent's
Canal from Little Venice, London Zoo and Camden Lock,
daily in summer and during weekends in winter.

Sightseeing

The best introduction to London for a first time visitor is one of the panoramic tours offered by several companies including London Transport, Cityrama, and London Pride. More detailed, guided tours are available from these companies and from Evan Evans, Frames, and London Crusader. These companies use blue badge registered guide trained by the London Visitor and Convention Bureau.

Culture Bus operates a fleet of yellow buses on a circular route stopping at the major sights. The ticket allows you to stop at as many of these as you wish in one day.

The best way to study London in detail and to get off the beaten track is to explore on foot. Several companies in membership of LVCB run walking tours usually starting at underground stations. No pre-booking is necessary. London events publications give details of daily walks.

For information on sightseeing, tour bookings and discount cards contact a tourist information centre, see list on back cover.

TRAVEL INFORMATION

London Transport
55 Broadway, London SW1 0BD
Tel: 01-222 1234 – All enquiries (24 hr service, seven days a week)
LT operates a number of Travel Information Centres which are open to personal callers only:

Underground Stations
Charing Cross – Mon-Fri 0815-1800
King's Cross – Daily 0815-1800
Oxford Circus – Mon-Sat 0815-1800
Piccadilly Circus – Daily 0815-2130
St James's Park – Mon-Fri 0815-1700
Victoria – Daily 0815-1800

British Rail Travel Centres
Provide comprehensive information on British Rail services/holidays etc. (for personal callers only)

Offices at principal stations
Paddington – Mon-Sat 0800-2000, Sun 0900-1630
Euston – Mon-Sat 0700-2300, Sun 0830-2300
King's Cross – Mon-Sat 0645-2300, Sun 0800-2300
St Pancras – Mon-Sat 0740-2100, Sun 0830-2100
Waterloo – Daily 0800-2200
London Bridge – Mon-Fri 0830-1830, Sat 0830-1400
Cannon Street – Mon-Fri 0800-1830
Charing Cross – Daily 0730-2000
Victoria – Daily 0730-2130

KENSINGTON AND CHELSEA

The Royal Borough of Kensington and Chelsea includes within its boundaries the areas of Brompton, Earl's Court, Knightsbridge and Notting Hill.

Kensington is of Anglo-Saxon origin and the name appears in the Domesday survey of 1086. Queen Victoria made it into a 'Royal' borough in 1901. From the early 17th century, large houses were built between Kensington High Street and Notting Hill Gate. Holland House in Holland Park is the oldest survivor, parts of which date from 1607.

Kensington Palace was the home of the reigning sovereigns from 1689 until 1760. It was the birthplace of Queen Victoria in 1819 and here she learnt in 1837 that she had become Queen. Today the State Apartments and Court Dress Collection are open to the public as are the grounds, even though several members of the Royal Family still live here, including Prince Charles and Princess Diana. Opposite the Palace are many embassies.

Queen Victoria's Consort, Prince Albert, provided the inspiration for the building of artistic and scientific institutions with the profits from the Great Exhibition of 1851. The Museums of South Kensington include the departments of the British Museum for Natural History, Science and Geology and the Victoria and Albert Museum. The Royal Albert Hall in Kensington Gore was completed in 1870 after Prince Albert's death, and is the venue of many concerts including the popular Henry Wood Promenade concerts. (See p. 24 – Westminster). Opposite is the striking memorial to Prince Albert.

The Notting Hill Carnival, held on the August Bank Holiday weekend in and around Portobello Road and Ladbroke Grove, was started by the Afro-Caribbean community which settled there in the 1950's.

Chelsea was also mentioned in the Domesday book. Henry VIII had a manor built by the Thames in Cheyne Walk where his daughter, later Queen Elizabeth I, spent part of her childhood. Chelsea Old Church, also in Cheyne Walk, stands on the site of a 12th century Norman church. It has associations with Sir Thomas More whose mansion was nearby.

The King's Road is Chelsea's thoroughfare extending from Sloane Square to Fulham. The eastern part was a private road created in the 1660's by King Charles II and used as a route out to Hampton Court Palace, hence the name. It is well known for its antique shops and fashion boutiques and is still a place to be seen and to see the latest trends, particularly on Saturdays.

continued overleaf

KENSINGTON AND CHELSEA

Charles II founded the Royal Hospital for veteran soldiers in 1682 to a design by Christopher Wren. The building is still occupied by old soldiers (affectionately known as 'Chelsea Pensioners') who wear traditional red coats. The Chelsea Flower Show takes place in the grounds of the Hospital in May.

Chelsea was the home of artists and writers and Thomas Carlyle's house can still be visited. The Chelsea Physic Garden was established in 1676 and the founding of the Chelsea Porcelain Works in 1745 further enhanced Chelsea's reputation. In 1902 the Chelsea Arts Club was formed. Founder members included Walter Sickert, Augustus John and Sir Alfred Munnings. Pop musicians and actors favour today's Chelsea which retains much of its residential quality.

The area of Knightsbridge dates from the 11th century. Today it is renowned for its smart shops in Beauchamp Place and Brompton Road. The most famous is 'Harrod's', one of the largest department stores in the world, which has occupied its present site on Brompton Road since 1905. The annual January and July sales are a huge attraction.

For further information on the borough of Kensington and Chelsea contact:
Town Hall, Hornton Street,
Kensington W8 7NX.
Tel: 01-937 5464.
Open: Mon-Fri 0900-1700.

Natural History Museum, S. Kensington

PLACES OF INTEREST

ART GALLERIES

Zamana Gallery (L)
1 Cromwell Gardens, SW7
Tel: 01-584 6612

Open: Mon-Thur 1000-1730, Sat 1000-1730, Sun 1330-1830
1987 2-18 Jan; 5 Feb-26 April; 18 May-30 Aug; 23 Sept-20 Dec. Closed Mon 1000-1730, Tues-Sat 1200-1730 Sun
Admission: Free
♿ Access
⊖ South Kensington

Bookshop and Exhibition Gallery in Islamic/Cultural Centre concentrating on Middle Eastern Art and Architecture.

MUSEUMS

Baden-Powell House (L)
Queen's Gate, SW7
Tel: 01-584 7030

Open: Jan-Dec daily 0900-2000
Admission: Free

⊖ South Kensington/Gloucester Road

Exhibition within a modern hostel tracing life history of Baden-Powell, founder of the Scout Association.

Commonwealth Institute (L)
Kensington High Street, W8
Tel: 01-603 4535

Admission: Free
♿ Access
⊖ High Street Kensington

There are exhibits illustrating life in some 40 Commonwealth countries; the Institute also presents a changing programme of thematic and artistic exhibitions: films, lectures, performances, restaurant and cafeteria.

Geological Museum
Exhibition Road, SW7
Tel: 01-589 3444

Open: Mon-Sat 1000-1800, Sun 1430-1800; closed New Year's Day, Good Friday, May Day Bank Holiday, 24-26 Dec inc.
Admission: Free – charges likely from 1987
♿ Access
⊖ South Kensington

The museum, a department of the British Museum, shows "The Story of the Earth" – an audio-visual display and general principles of geology. It contains a gem collection including rubies, sapphires, emeralds and diamonds – cut and uncut – and a piece of the Moon. Bookshop, lectures, films.

Museum of Instruments (Royal College of Music)
Prince Consort Road, South Kensington, SW7
Tel: 01-589 3643

Open: Wed during term time from 1100-1600
Admission: Charge

⊖ South Kensington

Almost 500 exhibits including the Donaldson Collection, string and wind instruments from the 16th-19th centuries with some instruments from Asia and Africa.

National Army Museum
Royal Hospital Road, Chelsea, SW3
Tel: 01-730 0717

Open: Mon-Sat 1000-1730, Sun 1400-1730; Closed 1 Jan, Good Friday, May Day Bank Holiday and over Christmas
Admission: Free
♿ Access
⊖ Sloane Square

The museum covers the history of the British Army throughout five centuries from 1485, the Indian Army up to independence in 1947 and colonial land forces. Bookshop, lectures, films.

National Sound Archive of the British Library
29 Exhibition Road, SW7
Tel: 01-589 6603

Open: Re-opening after building work early 1987 Mon-Fri 0930-1730 (Thurs 2100). (Advisable to make a listening appointment)
Admission: Free
⊖ South Kensington

The archive holds more than half a million discs of all kinds and more than 35,000 hours of recorded tape including collections of music, wildlife sounds, drama and spoken literature.

continued overleaf

KENSINGTON AND CHELSEA

Natural History Museum (L)
Cromwell Road, South Kensington, SW7
Tel: 01-589 6323

Open: Mon-Sat 1000-1800, Sun 1430-1800; Closed 24-26 Dec inc., New Year's Day, Good Friday, May Day Bank Holiday
Admission: Free (Charges from April 1987)
♿ Access
⊖ South Kensington

The museum is a department of the British Museum and features British natural history including pre-historic dinosaurs and the collection of whale skeletons; fossils of extinct European mammals; flora and fauna; man's place in evolution and human biology; minerals and meteorites. Models, films and games encourage participation. Lectures, bookshop, cafeteria.

Science Museum
Exhibition Road, SW7
Tel: 01-589 3456

Open: Mon-Sat 1000-1800, Sun 1430-1800; Closed 24-26 Dec inc, 1 Jan, Good Friday, May Day Bank Holiday
Admission: Free
♿ Access
⊖ South Kensington

The museum traces the development of power from wind to steam and nuclear energy; the history of transport from the wheel to spaceflights and includes a full-size replica of the Apollo II Lunar Lander, the development of computers with participatory exhibits. The Wellcome Museum of the History of Medicine moved here in 1982. Models, lectures, films, bookshop, cafeteria.

Victoria and Albert Museum (L)
Cromwell Road, SW7
Tel: 01-589 6371

Open: Mon-Thu, and Sat 1000-1750, Sun 1430-1750; Closed Fri and 24-26 Dec, New Year's Day, May Day Bank Holiday and Good Friday
Admission Charge: Voluntary donation
♿ Access
⊖ South Kensington

London's major museum of applied art with collections representing a wide variety of cultures. The exhibits are grouped in periods from Early Mediaeval to English Art of the 19th century, showing sculpture, paintings, textiles, furniture; the famous Raphael Cartoons in Room 48 are on loan to the V & A from the Queen. The Costume collection includes fashion through the ages. The Henry Cole Wing added in 1982 shows paintings, drawings and photography. The Boilerhouse Project (seep p. 52) is now closed and is due to open in Butler's Wharf in 1988. The space will be used by the V & A from January 1987. Lectures, films, tours, bookshop, restaurant.

HISTORIC HOUSES/BUILDINGS

Carlyle's House (L)
24 Cheyne Row, SW3
Tel: 01-352 7087

Open: 1 April-31 Oct, Wed-Sun & Bank Holiday Monday 1100-1700 (last admission 1630); Closed Good Friday
Admission: Charge
⊖ Sloane Square then Bus 11

Queen Anne terraced house occupied by the writer Thomas Carlyle from 1834-1881. Leading intellectuals and writers visited Carlyle here including Dickens, Ruskin and Tennyson. (No electricity).

Crosby Hall
Cheyne Walk, SW3
Tel: 01-352 9663

Open: Daily (unless Hall in use for private functions) 1000-1200, 1415-1700 (Mon-Sat), 1415-1700 (Sun); Closed for approximately one week at Christmas

⊖ Sloane Square, South Kensington

The 15th century dining hall of Crosby Hall, a mansion in Bishopsgate, moved to this site in 1910, formerly Sir Thomas More's garden. It retains its original roof, Oriel window and fireplace.

Royal Hospital, Chelsea

KENSINGTON AND CHELSEA

art. The Arab Hall – the most unusual feature – is based on Moorish-Spanish design. The paintings, drawings and sculpture include works by Leighton, Burne-Jones and Millais. Recitals.

Linley Sambourne House
18 Stafford Terrace, W8
Tel: 01-994 1019

Open: Wed 1000-1600, Sun 1400-1700, 1 March-31 Oct
Admission: Charge
⊖ High Street Kensington

Home of Linley Sambourne, chief political cartoonist of Punch. The furnishing and decoration reflect the artistic taste of the 1880s, and is maintained by the Victorian Society. Also on show are cartoons and photographs by Sambourne and his friends.

Royal Hospital Chelsea
Royal Hospital Road, Chelsea, SW3
Tel: 01-730 0161

Open: Weekdays: 1000-1200 & 1400-1600, Sun (April-Sep) 1400-1600
Admission: Free
⊖ Sloane Square

Built by Sir Christopher Wren 1682-1692 as the home for retired soldiers – Chelsea Pensioners; the Great Chapel, Hall and Museum are of particular interest.

CHURCHES

Brompton Oratory
Brompton Road, SW3
Tel: 01-589 4811

Open: Daily 0700-2000
⊖ South Kensington

A richly decorated Italianate church, built to the designs of Herbert Gribble, first opened in 1884. It contains a magnificent Italian altarpiece and until 1903 (see p. 23), was the centre of the Roman Catholic Church in London.

Kensington Palace State Apartments
Kensington Gardens, W8
Tel: 01-937 9561

Open: 1 Jan-31 Dec, Mon-Sat 0900-1700, Sun 1300-1700; last tickets 1615
Admission: Charge
⊖ Queensway, Kensington High Street

Kensington Palace, a 17th century mansion rebuilt by Wren and Hawksmoor was the main royal residence from 1689 to 1760. The State Apartments, restored and furnished from the Royal Collection, recreate the Stuart/Hanoverian periods and include paintings by Lely, Van Dyck, carvings by Grinling Gibbons; Queen Victoria's suite occupied by her as a princess includes her bedchamber; the Court Dress Collection opened in 1984 with uniforms and costumes from the 18th to 20th century.
Members of the Royal Family still occupy the private apartments.

Leighton House Museum and Art Gallery
12 Holland Park Road, W14
Tel: 01-602 3316

Open: Mon-Sat 1100-1700 (1800 during exhibitions)
Admission: Free
⊖ High Street Kensington

Designed by Lord Leighton in 1866, the House contains rooms furnished in period style and a permanent exhibition of Victorian

continued overleaf

11

KENSINGTON AND CHELSEA

Chelsea Old Church (All Saints)
Old Church Street, Cheyne Walk, SW3
Tel: 01-352 5637

⊖ Sloane Square then bus 11, 22

Built on the site of a Norman church, Chelsea Old Church was probably founded in the 12th century. It suffered severe damage in the Second World War and was restored and rededicated in 1958. It has associations with Sir Thomas More who lived in Chelsea and worshipped here. In 1528 he restored the Chapel which dates from 1325.

PARKS, GARDENS AND OPEN SPACES

Chelsea Physic Garden
66 Royal Hospital Road, SW3
Tel: 01-352 5646

Open: 12 April-18 Oct, Wed, Sun and Bank Holidays 1400-1700; 19 May-22 May inc (Chelsea Flower Show Week) 1200-1700; appointment only at other times
Admission: Charge

♿ Access

⊖ Sloane Square

This is the second oldest Physic garden in the country and was founded in 1673 by the Apothecaries Society for botanical investigation and education; it includes a herb garden, the oldest rock garden in the country, and a statue of Sir Hans Sloane – its founder.

Holland Park
New Lodge, Holland House, Kensington, W8
Tel: 01-602 2226

♿ Access

⊖ High Street Kensington, Holland Park

Wooded park with wild areas and animals; flower gardens. Only a wing remains of the Jacobean Mansion of Holland House, now a youth hostel. Orangery with changing exhibitions. Open-air theatre and concerts in summer. Cafeteria, restaurant.

Kensington Gardens, W8
Tel: 01-937 4848

⊖ Queensway, Lancaster Gate, High Street Kensington

Once the private gardens of Kensington Palace, now a 274 acre park linked with Hyde Park. The Round Pond, the Orangery, built by Hawksmoor and Vanbrugh, the Sunken Gardens and the statue of Peter Pan, are special features.

The Flower Walk leads to the Albert Memorial opposite the Royal Albert Hall commissioned by Queen Victoria after the Prince Consort's death in 1861 and designed by Sir George Gilbert-Scott. Artists and writers decorate the pedestal and the four continents as well as industry are represented.

Roof Gardens (L)
99 Kensington High Street, W8
Tel: 01-937 7994

Open: Mon-Fri 0930-1800 (can close at short notice for private functions)
Admission: Free

⊖ High Street Kensington

The Roof Gardens were part of the Derry and Toms department store built in 1930; this has now been converted into the Kensington Exhibition Centre and Rainbow Suite; ornamental flower beds, flamingos and other birds inhabit the roof-top gardens; which also include a fashionable disco.

SPORTS CENTRES

Chelsea Sports Centre
Chelsea Manor Street, SW3
Tel: 01-352 6985

⊖ Sloane Square

Indoor sports centre with swimming pool, sauna, gym, spa bath and solarium.

Kensington New Pools
Walmer Road, W11
Tel: 01-727 9923

⊖ Ladbroke Grove

Indoor sports hall, multi-gym, swimming pool, solarium, sauna and outdoor sports ground.

SHOPPING

Principal areas are Kensington High Street (⊖ High Street Kensington), King's Road (⊖ Sloane Square then Bus 11), and Knightsbridge – for Harrods, Harvey Nichols and Beauchamp Place (⊖ Knightsbridge).

KENSINGTON AND CHELSEA

MARKETS

Antiquarius
135 Kings Road, Chelsea, SW3
Open: Mon-Sat 1000-1800
⊖ Sloane Square
Covered antique market, also antique fashion goods.

Chenil Galleries (L)
181 Kings Road, SW3
Open: Mon-Sat 1000-1800
⊖ Sloane Square
Covered antique market.

Earls Court Exhibition Centre Sunday Market (L)
Lillie Road, SW6
Open: Sun 1000-1500
⊖ Earls Court
Antiques; foodstuffs; bric-a-brac; clothes.

Portobello Road, W11
Open: Mon-Thurs 0900-1600 (approx.) Fri & Sat 0800-1700 (approx.)
⊖ Ladbroke Grove/Notting Hill Gate
Clothes; food (Mon-Sat); bric-a-brac; flea market (Fri & Sat); antiques (Sat only). Includes Grays Portobello and Roger's Antique Gallery, both covered.

Kensington Market (L)
Kensington High Street, W8
Open: Mon-Sat 1000-1800
⊖ High Street Kensington
Fashion.

WESTMINSTER

The City of Westminster is the seat of national government and includes within its boundaries some of the most important buildings in Britain. It is London's commercial and entertainment centre and yet it contains over one hundred acres of parkland. The City of Westminster stretches from Hampstead in the north to the Thames in the south.

There is evidence that the Romans made the first settlement at Westminster in AD 43. During the 7th to 9th centuries, ships landed here. During this time Westminster Abbey was founded and all English monarchs have been crowned here since 1066.

The boundaries of the City of Westminster were defined as early as 1222 and the area was established in the 14th century as the seat of Government. The Palace of Westminster was the first residence of sovereigns until Henry VIII moved to Whitehall Palace. Of this old building, only the Banqueting House survives. Whitehall today is still dominated by Government offices, including the Ministry of Defence and the Treasury. Perhaps the best known of all the buildings in the area is the official residence of Prime Ministers since 1732 – Number 10 Downing Street, just off Whitehall.

Covent Garden is not just a popular shopping area but has a long history as the convent garden of Westminster Abbey. The Russell family took over the land in the 16th century and commissioned Inigo Jones to design a continental-style piazza. The Covent Garden fruit and vegetable market was established from 1670. By 1974 the market had outgrown its surroundings and was resited at Nine Elms in Battersea. The old market buildings were restored; in the Flower Market is the London Transport Museum, to be followed by the Theatre Museum in April 1987. Shops, restaurants and wine bars occupy the Central Market and market stalls sell antiques, crafts and general goods. Free entertainment and music is a delightful feature of the piazza in front of St. Paul's Church. A lively annual event is the Festival of Street Theatre in June.

The church, also designed by Inigo Jones, is commonly known as "The Actors' Church". Plaques inside the church commemorate celebrated actors and memorial services for people from the theatrical world are often held here. Both the Theatre Royal Drury Lane and the Royal Opera House are in the area, established after the Restoration in 1660, when King Charles II came to the throne. His mistress, Nell Gwynne, appeared at the Theatre Royal Drury Lane.

London's theatre-land spread and Shaftesbury Avenue, completed in 1886, took over as the centre for theatrical entertainment. In all, there are thirty-four theatres in the City of Westminster and many more cinemas. The larger ones in Leicester Square are often chosen for royal charity première film performances. (See theatre list on p. 26).

Soho is a cosmopolitan area with a good choice of restaurants. It has a large Chinese community with an officially designated "China Town" centred around Gerrard Street. In February, the Chinese New year is celebrated here with processions and lion dances.

The major department stores are to be found along Oxford Street, which was first developed as a shopping street in the 19th century, and along Regent Street. Nearby is Bond Street, noted for its more exclusive shops specialising in fashion, jewellery and antiques. Sotheby's, the fine art auctioneers, have a showroom here.

Within the City of Westminster's northern corner lies St. John's Wood, associated with that most traditional English sport, cricket, which has been played at St. John's Wood since 1787 when Lord's Cricket Ground was founded by Thomas Lord. Nearby is the area of St. Marylebone, home of Harley Street, Sherlock Holmes and Madame Tussaud's.

A large area of London was redeveloped in the early 19th century by the architect John Nash under the patronage of

Covent Garden

continued overleaf

WESTMINSTER

the Prince Regent, later King George IV. Regent Street was designed to link the Regent's residence in Westminster with Regent's Park. The Regent's Canal opened in 1820 and London Zoo was founded in 1824. Today, the Canal waterbus service from Little Venice to London Zoo recreates travel in a different era of London's history.

Piccadilly Circus, with its statue of Eros at the southern end of Shaftesbury Avenue, is one of London's most famous landmarks. The name Piccadilly is derived from a tailor who once lived here selling frilling for collars called "Picadils". From 1760, members of the aristocracy built smart town houses attracted by the proximity of Green Park. Today, they have been replaced by offices although some of the gentlemen's clubs survive in the area of St. James's.

Restaurants, entertainment and late night shopping are under one roof at the Trocadero Centre in Piccadilly Circus, which opened in 1985. It houses the Guinness World of Records Exhibition, Light Fantastic Holographic Gallery, and the London Experience – an audio visual show. The London Pavilion Cinema is being restored as a shopping and entertainment centre, linked to the Trocadero.

Mayfair, named after a 17th century cattle fair held in May, was developed in the 1730's to accommodate members of the aristocracy who were connected with the nearby St. James' Palace. Belgravia was another haunt of the gentry. Thomas Cubitt designed the squares, the largest being Belgrave Square, linked by wide roads. Today, embassies occupy many of the grand houses although it is still largely a residential area, part of the Grosvenor Estate owned by the Duke of Westminster, whose ancestors also developed Pimlico and Mayfair.

London's most famous Royal residence is Buckingham Palace, which started life as Buckingham House, built by the First Duke of Buckingham in the beginning of the 18th century. George IV later bought it and after alteration it became Buckingham Palace. The Changing the Guard ceremony which takes place in the Palace courtyard daily in the summer (on alternate days in the Winter) is on most visitors' itinerary.

Among the many events in the City of Westminster are Trooping the Colour (the Queen's official Birthday Parade), and the Beating Retreat Ceremony in Horse Guards Parade off Whitehall, which both take place in June. One of the biggest state occasions is the State Opening of Parliament in late October or early November. The City of Westminster also organises local events and festivals.

For further information contact: Westminster City Hall, Victoria Street, SW1E 6QP. Tel: 01-828-8070. Open: Mon-Fri 0830-1630.

PLACES OF INTEREST

WESTMINSTER

ART GALLERIES/CENTRES

British Crafts Centre (L)
43 Earlham Street, WC2
Tel: 01-836 6993
Open: Mon-Fri 1000-1730, Sat 1100-1700; Closed Public Holidays
Admission: Free
🚇 Covent Garden

Changing and permanent display of contemporary British crafts for sale chosen from work by members of the British Crafts Centre Bookstall.

Crafts Council Gallery
12 Waterloo Place, SW1
Tel: 01-930 4811
Open: Tue-Sat 1000-1700, Sun 1400-1700
Admission: Charge
♿ Access
🚇 Piccadilly Circus/Charing Cross

Series of exhibitions of high quality contemporary and historical craft. Bookstall, information centre with slide library.

Design Centre
28 Haymarket, SW1
Tel: 01-839 8000
Open: Mon & Tue 1000-1800, Wed-Fri 1000-2000, Sun 1300-1800
Admission: Free
🚇 Piccadilly Circus

Changing exhibitions of British design in the consumer, contract and engineering fields. Shop with souvenirs designed and made in Britain.

Institute of Contemporary Arts
Nash House, The Mall, SW1
Tel: 01-930 3647
Open: Daily 1200-2300
Admission: Charge
🚇 Charing Cross/Piccadilly Circus

The gallery is on the ground floor of a terrace of grand private houses designed in the 1830s by architect John Nash. Three galleries show contemporary art; exhibitions change approximately every 6 weeks; cinema, video library, theatre, restaurant and bar.

Light Fantastic Gallery of Holography (L)
48 South Row, Covent Garden, WC2
Tel: 01-836 6423/6424
Open: Mon-Wed 1000-1800, Thu-Fri 1000-2000, Sat 1000-1900, Sun 1100-1800
Admission: Charge
🚇 Covent Garden/Leicester Square/Charing Cross

Permanent gallery with a selection of white light holography from all over the world. Special exhibitions.

Light Fantastic – World Centre of Holography (L)
1st Floor, The Trocadero, 13 Coventry Street, W1
Tel: 01-836 6423
Open: Daily 1000-2200
Admission: Charge
🚇 Piccadilly Circus/Leicester Square

8000 square feet devoted to world's best holograms plus applications in industry, medicine, science.

Mall Galleries (L)
The Mall, SW1
Tel: 01-930 6845
Open: 1000-1700 Daily (during exhibitions)
♿ Access
🚇 Charing Cross/Piccadilly Circus

Changing exhibitions of contemporary art, mainly by British artists in traditional media.

National Gallery
Trafalgar Square, WC2
Tel: 01-839 3321
Open: Mon-Sat 1000-1800, Sun 1400-1800; Closed 24-25 Dec, New Year's Day, Good Friday and May Day
Admission: Free
♿ Access
🚇 Charing Cross/Leicester Square

The National Gallery founded in 1824 is one of the world's greatest art galleries with a collection representing European art through the centuries. The works of major painters include Constable, Reynolds, Turner, Rembrandt, Van Dyck, Claude, Poussin, Cezanne, Gaugin, Monet, Pissarro, Botticelli, Leonardo da Vinci, Canaletto, Goya and Velasquez. Lectures, tours, audio-visual programmes, cafeteria.

continued overleaf

17

WESTMINSTER

National Portrait Gallery
St. Martin's Place, WC2
Tel: 01-930 1552
Open: Mon-Fri 1000-1700, Sat 1000-1800, Sun 1400-1800; Closed Good Friday, May Day Bank Holiday, 24-26 Dec inc., New Year's Day
Admission: Charge for some exhibitions
♿ Access
⊖ Charing Cross/Leicester Square

Collection of portraits of famous men and women from the Tudors to the present day including paintings, sculpture, engravings and photographs.

Queen's Gallery (L)
Buckingham Palace Road, SW1
Tel: 01-930 3007 Ext. 430
Open: Tue-Sat 1100-1700, Sun 1400-1700; Closed Mon except Bank Holidays
Admission: Charge
♿ Access
⊖ Victoria/St. James's Park

Formerly the Palace chapel, now a gallery with exhibitions from the Royal collection.

Royal Academy of Arts
Burlington House, Piccadilly, W1
Tel: 01-734 9052
Open: Daily 1000-1800
Admission: Charge
♿ Access
⊖ Piccadilly Circus/Green Park

Burlington House – a private mansion of 1665 – was rebuilt in 1873 to provide a home for many learned societies including the Royal Academy of Arts founded in 1768. There are changing exhibitions in four main galleries including a permanent collection. The "open" Summer Exhibition from May-August each year shows the work of amateurs and professionals, chosen by committee.

Saatchi Collection
98A Boundary Road, NW8
Tel: 01-624 8299
Open: Fri & Sat 1200-1800. Telephone in advance
Admission: Free
⊖ St. John's Wood

A former paint warehouse with changing exhibitions from the Saatchi Collection of contemporary art.

Serpentine Gallery
Kensington Gardens, W2
Tel: 01-402 6075
Open: Spring & Autumn, 1000-1700; Summer, 1000-1800; Winter, 1000-1600
Admission: Free
⊖ Lancaster Gate/Knightsbridge

Changing exhibitions of the works of contemporary artists are organised by the Arts Council in this converted cafeteria.

Tate Gallery
Millbank, SW1
Tel: 01-821 1313
Open: Mon-Sat 1000-1750, Sun 1400-1750; Closed 24-26 Dec, New Year's Day, Good Friday, May Day Holiday
Admission: Free (admission charge for special exhibitions)
♿ Access
⊖ Pimlico

The Tate Gallery founded in 1897 houses the national collection of British painting as well as contemporary European, American and British works. Reynolds, Gainsborough, Constable and the Pre-Raphaelites are well represented. Changing exhibitions of modern art. Clore Gallery will open in Spring 1987 and show the extensive Turner Bequest of some 200 finished oil paintings and thousands of drawings. Lectures, tours, films. Cafeteria and famous Restaurant

Wallace Collection
Hertford House, Manchester Square, W1
Tel: 01-935 0687
Open: Mon-Sat 1000-1700, Sun 1400-1700; Closed 24-26 Dec inc, New Year's Day, Good Friday, May Day Bank Holiday
Admission: Free
♿ Access
⊖ Bond Street

The gallery opened in 1900 in the former home of the Marquess of Hertford showing the family's collection of art and furniture bequeathed to the nation. Amongst the masterpieces are works by Rembrandt, Hals, Rubens, Murillo and Van Dyck. Also 18th century furniture, porcelain, goldsmiths work, Oriental and European arms. Bookshop.

MUSEUMS

Cabinet War Rooms
Clive Steps, King Charles Street, SW1
Tel: 01-930 6961
Open: Daily 1000-1750 (last admission 1715), also Easter Mon, Spring & Autumn Bank Holiday; Closed Mon, 24-26 Dec, New Year's Day, Good Friday, May Bank Holiday
Admission: Charge
♿ Access
🚇 Westminster

A suite of 19 historic rooms, including Cabinet Room, Transatlantic Telephone Room, Map Room and Churchill's Room, which were in operational use during the Second World War.

Cricket Memorial Gallery (L)
Lord's Ground, NW8
Tel: 01-289 1611
Open: Mon-Sat 1030-1700 on match days only. Appointment required other days
♿ Access
🚇 St. John's Wood

The history of cricket is covered from earliest times to the present day. It includes paintings, trophies and the Ashes.

Faraday's Laboratory and Museum
21 Albemarle Street, W1
Tel: 01-409 2992
Open: Tue & Thu 1300-1600; Closed Bank Holidays
Admission: Charge
🚇 Green Park

Restored 19th century magnetic laboratory of Michael Faraday with an adjacent display of his apparatus, belongings and notebooks.

London Toy and Model Museum (L)
21-23 Craven Hill, W2
Tel: 01-262 9450/7905
Open: Tue-Sat 1000-1730, Sun & Bank Holiday Monday 1100-1730; Closed Christmas Day, New Year's Day, Monday (Ex Bank Holiday)
Admission: Charge
🚇 Lancaster Gate/Queensway/Paddington

Extensive collections of commercially-made toys and models from 1850 onwards – including trains, cars, planes, nursery toys, etc. Garden with working railway. Bookshop, special exhibitions, cafeteria.

London Transport Museum (L)
Covent Garden, WC2
Tel: 01-379 6344
Open: Every day 1000-1800, last admission 1715; Closed 24, 25, 26 Dec
Admission: Charge
♿ Access
🚇 Covent Garden/Leicester Square

The history of public transport in London: Horse buses, motor buses, trolleybuses, trams and underground trains. Unique working displays, video programmes. Free entry to Museum Shop. Lectures. Cafeteria.

Museum of Mankind
6 Burlington Gardens, W1
Tel: 01-437 2224
Open: Mon-Sat 1000-1700, Sun 1430-1800; Closed 24-27 Dec, 1 Jan, Good Friday & May Day
Admission: Free
🚇 Piccadilly Circus/Green Park

Ethnographic department of the British Museum with collections from Africa, Australia and the Pacific Islands, North and South America; exhibitions on different cultures and peoples.

Pollock's Toy Museum
1 Scala Street, W1
Tel: 01-636 3452
Open: Mon-Sat 1000-1700
Admission: Charge
🚇 Goodge Street

The house dates from 1760 and contains toys of all kinds – dolls, dolls' houses, Victorian nursery, toy theatres, teddy bears, tin toys and folk toys from around the world. Toy shop.

continued overleaf

WESTMINSTER

WESTMINSTER

Theatre Museum
Russell Street, WC2
Tel: 01-836 7891

Provisional opening hours (from end April 1987). Tues-Sat 1100-1900 Gallery and Theatre; Tues-Sat 1100-2000 Shop, Cafe and Ticket Master facilities; Sun 1100-1900 Shop, Cafe and Ticket Master facilities

Admission: Charge

⊖ Covent Garden

London's long awaited Theatre Museum is due to open, appropriately on Shakespeare's birthday; 23 April, 1987. The Museum occupies the same building as the London Transport Museum in Russell Street, Covent Garden, providing a permanent home for the collections that have made up the theatre department of the Victoria and Albert Museum since 1974. The new museum will become a major centre for students of the performing arts. There are three exhibition galleries, one contains a semi-permanent display of the story of the performing arts with exhibits drawn from the Museum's own collections which include costume, jewellery, props, engravings and playbills. A second gallery named in honour of Sir John Gielgud will have temporary exhibitions on particular themes. The third gallery is for paintings. The 85 seat auditorium can be used for various events including lectures, workshops and performances. In addition there is a cafe and shop and "Ticket Master" theatre booking facilities.

HISTORIC BUILDINGS/HOUSES

Apsley House
149 Piccadilly, W1
Tel: 01-499 5676

Open: Tue-Thu, Sat 1000-1800, Sun 1430-1800

Admission: Charge

⊖ Hyde Park Corner

Built between 1771 and 1778, Apsley House was the home of the first Duke of Wellington, on show are Wellington relics, Sèvres porcelain and silver. The original address was Number 1, London.

Banqueting House
Horse Guards Avenue, Whitehall, SW1
Tel: 01-930 4179

Open: 2 Jan-31 Dec, Tue-Sat 1000-1730, Sun 1400-1730; Closed New Year's Day, 25 & 26 Dec, Good Friday & at short notice for Government functions

⊖ Westminster/Charing Cross

Banqueting House is the only remains of the old Whitehall Palace designed by Inigo Jones and completed in 1622. Charles I was beheaded outside in 1649. Rubens ceilings.

House of St. Barnabas-in-Soho
1 Greek Street, Soho, W1
Tel: 01-437 1894

Open: Wed 1430-1615, Thu 1100-1230; Closed Christmas & Easter

Admission: Free (donations welcome)

⊖ Tottenham Court Road

Georgian rooms and architecture, garden (Mulberry Tree), Victorian copy of 13th century French Gothic Chapel.

Houses of Parliament
Parliament Square, SW1
Tel: 01-219 3090/3100

Admission: Free

⊖ Westminster

The Palace of Westminster in late Gothic style was designed by Sir Charles Barry and completed in 1850. The building has been recently cleaned to reveal the sandstone colour and detailed sculpture work. Visits to the Palace of Westminster and Westminster Hall can only be made by prior arrangement directly with a Member of Parliament or Peer (Visitors from abroad should contact their Embassy; there is usually a long waiting list). To watch a debate:
House of Commons:
Queue outside St. Stephen's entrance; Admission from 1615 Mon-Thurs; from 1000 Fri, to the Strangers Gallery.
House of Lords:
Queue at same entrance; Admission from 1430, Tues, Wed, Thurs and some Mons.

Jewel Tower
Old Palace Yard, Westminster, SW1
Tel: 01-222 2219

Open: 15 March-15 Oct, Mon-Sat 0930-1830; 16 Oct-14 March, 0930-1600

Admission: Free

⊖ Westminster

14th century tower of Mediaeval Palace of Westminster; Edward III built this moated tower to store his personal jewels; also assay office.

WESTMINSTER

Royal Courts of Justice
Strand, WC2
Tel: 01-936 6000
Open: Mon-Fri 1000-1600
Admission: Free
♿ Access
⊖ Temple/Chancery Lane

Victorian Gothic architecture opened in 1882. Legal costume exhibition situated at main entrance. Minimum age for entry to courts is 17 years.

PLACES OF INTEREST

Guinness World of Records (L)
Trocadero Centre, Piccadilly, W1
Tel: 01-439 7331
Open: Daily 1000-2200; Closed Christmas Day
Admission: Charge
♿ Access
⊖ Piccadilly Circus/Leicester Square

An exhibition using models, videos, computers and electronic displays to bring to life the Guiness Book of Records.

Laserium (L)
London Planetarium, Marylebone Road, NW1
Tel: 01-486 1121
Open: Most evenings throughout the year. Details Tel: 01-486 2242
Admission: Charge
⊖ Baker Street

Laser light concerts combining dazzling displays of the laser beam with rock and classical music.

London Diamond Centre (L)
10 Hanover Street, W1
Tel: 01-629 5511
Open: 0930-1730 Mon-Fri All year, 0930-1330 Sat
Admission: Charge
⊖ Oxford Circus

Exhibition shows diamonds from mining through to polishing. Showroom of diamonds and jewellery.

London Experience (L)
Trocadero Centre, Piccadilly Circus, W1
Tel: 01-439 4938
Open: Sun-Thu 1020-2220, Fri, Sat 1020-2300
Admission: Charge
♿ Access
⊖ Piccadilly Circus

30 minute audio visual show featuring the history, sights and sounds of London from Roman times to present day.

London Planetarium (L)
Marylebone Road, NW1
Tel: 01-486 1121
Open: Daily from 1100-1630; Closed Christmas Day
Admission: Charge (combined ticket available with Madame Tussauds)
⊖ Baker Street

The Astronomers' Gallery, features astronomers and their discoveries. Star show performances in the Planetarium.

Houses of Parliament

continued overleaf

WESTMINSTER

The Royal Mews

Madame Tussauds (L)
Marylebone Road, NW1
Tel: 01-935 6861
Open: Daily 1000-1730; Doors open earlier every weekend, Bank Holidays & during Summer season; Closed Christmas Day
Admission: Charge (combined ticket available with Planetarium)
♿ Access
⊖ Baker Street

World-famous collection of wax figures first opened in 1884. Exhibits include historical scenes, life size reconstruction of Nelson's flagship, Chamber of Horrors, New "Super Stars", political figures and international celebrities. The Royal Family.

Royal Mews (L)
Buckingham Palace Road, SW1
Tel: 01-930 4832 Ext. 634
Open: Wed & Thu 1400-1600; Closed during Ascot week, if Carriage Procession or Bank Holiday fall on an open day
Admission: Charge
♿ Access
⊖ Victoria

The Royal Mews houses the carriages of the Royal household and the Queen's horses. On view is the Golden Coronation Coach of 1761 and the Glass Coach used for Royal Weddings (including those of Prince Charles and Prince Andrew).

St. Catherine's House (General Register Office)
10 Kingsway, WC2
Tel: 01-242 0262
Open: Mon-Fri 0830-1630
♿ Access
⊖ Temple/Holborn

The Public Search Room contains indexes to the entries of all births, deaths and marriages which have taken place since 1 July 1837. For a fee, members of the public can obtain copies of certificates (two days' notice required).

CHURCHES

Guards Chapel
Wellington Barracks, Birdcage Walk, SW1
Tel: 01-930 4466
Open: Tue-Fri 1000-1500, Sun 0900-1230
Admission: Free
♿ Access
⊖ St. James's Park/Victoria

Built 1835. Bombed in 1944. Re-built 1960. Memorial Books. Household Division Regimental Chapels. Colours & Standards.

St. Clement Danes Church
Strand, WC2
Tel: 01-242 8282
Open: Mon-Sat 0800-1700, Sun 0800-1630
⊖ Temple

The church dates from 1022 AD; seafaring Danes settled here at the time of Alfred the Great. It was dedicated to St. Clement, patron saint of sailors. Rebuilt by Sir Christopher Wren in 1679, and has a pulpit attributed to Grinling Gibbons. Today, central church of the Royal Air Force with a memorial to the air forces of the Commonwealth and books of remembrance containing the names of airmen killed in the Second World War.

St. James's Church
197 Piccadilly, W1
Tel: 01-437 6023
Open: Mon-Sat 1000-1800, Sun 1200-1800; Closed Christmas Day
⊖ Piccadilly Circus

This is the only Wren church outside the City (1684). A collection of facsimile mediaeval church brasses are available for brass rubbings (charge). Cafeteria. Lectures. Recitals. Market.

WESTMINSTER

St. Margaret's Church
Parliament Square, Westminster, SW1
Tel: 01-222 6382
Open: Weekdays 0930-1600, Sun 1300-1600 and services
Admission: Free
⊖ Westminster/St. James's

A fine 16th century building with notable mediaeval and modern stained glass. Burial place of Sir Walter Raleigh. Parish church of the House of Commons.

St. Martin-in-the-Fields Church
Trafalgar Square, WC2
Tel: 01-930 0089
Open: Daily 0800-2000, except during services
Admission: Free
⊖ Charing Cross

Historic James Gibbs church built 1722-24 with Italian plaster-work and ceiling. Charles II was baptised and his mistress Nell Gwynne's burial is recorded here. The world renowned Academy of St. Martin-in-the-Fields orchestra was founded here and lunchtime concerts are a regular feature.

Westminster Abbey
Parliament Square, SW1
Tel: 01-222 5152
Open: Chapels, Poet's Corner, Choir, Statesmans, Aisle: Weekdays 0800-1800 (Wed 0800-1945). Visiting in Nave Sundays between services. Services as advertised
Admission: Charge (Nave and precincts free)
♿ Access
⊖ Westminster/St. James's Park

Abbey on this site since 8th century; present building dates from 13th century when it became Royal burial place. The towers were added by Hawksmoor in 1739, then restored by Wren. Coronations have taken place here since 1297. Special features: Grave of Unknown Warrior, Royal Tombs and Shrine of St. Edward the Confessor, Coronation Chair, Stone of Scone, Henry VII Chapel and Poets' Corner. An exhibition of Abbey Treasures is currently being assembled in three exhibition rooms in the Cloisters: the Chapter House, the Pyx Chapel and the Norman Undercroft. The Pyx Chapel, due to open in early 1987, will be the Treasury and contain plate from Westminster Abbey and St. Margaret's Church; the Norman Undercroft, due to open in the Spring of 1987, will contain effigies of well known figures including Admiral Lord Nelson.

Westminster Cathedral
Ashley Place, SW1
Tel: 01-834 7452
Open: Daily 0700-2000, Christmas Day 0700-1530
Admission: Charge to Cathedral Tower
♿ Access
⊖ Victoria/St. James's Park

Completed in 1903, the cathedral contains mosaics by Boris Anrep, Bronze of Teresa of Lisieux by Manzu, 14th century alabaster statue of our Lady of Westminster. Marbles from 100 countries. (Most important Catholic church in Britain, seat of Cardinal of Westminster.) It is possible to go to the top of the tower by lift.

continued overleaf

Royal Albert Hall

ENTERTAINMENT

Royal Albert Hall
Kensington Gore, SW7
Tel: 01-589 8212

Box office open: Mon-Sat 1000-1800, Sun 1000-1800 (approx) for the evening's performance

♿ Access

⊖ South Kensington/High Street Kensington

Built in 1871, impressive terracotta frieze – 270ft long. Tours of building in Summer. Sir Henry Wood Promenade Concerts held annually from mid-July to mid-Sept. Capacity: 4,000-7,000.

St. John's Smith Square
Smith Square, SW1
Tel: 01-222 2168

Open: Mon-Fri 1100-1800

⊖ Westminster/St. James's

18th century Thomas Archer Baroque Church. Restored after war damage, opened as concert hall 1969. Restaurant, bar and art gallery in crypt.

MARKETS

Berwick Street, W1
Open: Mon-Sat 0900-1700. Best times: Lunch-time

⊖ Bond Street

Food; clothes; household goods

Bond Street Antique Centre (L)
124 New Bond Street, W1
Open: Mon-Fri 1000-1745; Sat 1000-1600

⊖ Bond Street

Covered antique market.

Church Street
Off Lisson Grove, NW8
Open: Mon-Sat 0900-1700. Best times: Sat

⊖ Edgware Road

Fruit; veg; household goods; also antiques. With Alfies Antique market (covered) in Church Street.

Grays Antique Market (L)
58 Davies Street, W1
Open: Mon-Fri 1000-1800

⊖ Bond Street

Covered antiques market.

Grays Mews Antique Market (L)
1-7 Davies Mews, W1
Open: Mon-Fri 1000-1800

⊖ Bond Street

Covered antiques market.

Jubilee Market
Covent Garden, WC2
Open: Mon 0600-1800 Tue-Fri 0900-1600 Sat & Sun 0900-1700

⊖ Covent Garden

Antiques (Mon only); crafts; clothes; food (Tues-Fri), hand-made crafts (Sat & Sun). The Apple Market sells crafts (Tues-Sat) and antiques (Mon 1000-1900).

PARKS AND OPEN SPACES

Westminster has many squares which provide a tranquil retreat from the bustle of the city, and there are many large parks in Westminster making London one of the greenest capital cities in the world.

Green Park
⊖ Green Park

Green Park's 53 acre expanse consists of grassland and trees, no flowers – it may have been a burial ground. Pictures are for sale along the Piccadilly railings on Sundays.

Hyde Park
⊖ Marble Arch/Hyde Park Corner

The largest of London's parks covering 361 acres, Hyde Park was used as a hunting ground by Henry VIII. Its main feature is the Serpentine Lake which separates it from Kensington Gardens. There is a lido, re-opening in June 1987. In days gone by, Rotten Row, a corruption of Route du Roi, was the place to be seen riding, and today riders can still be seen cantering here, but joggers are more common. Speakers Corner (by Marble Arch) draws the crowds on Sundays – more political and less good-natured than in its golden days.

St. James Park
⊖ St. James Park

The oldest park in London and one of the most attractive with its beautiful flower beds. It covers 93 acres and many varieties of waterfowl thrive in the artificial lake and breed on Duck Island.

WESTMINSTER

Regents Park
🚇 Regents Park/Camden Town

Originally part of the forest of Middlesex, in the mid 16th century an area was set aside as an enclosed hunting park for Elizabeth I. In the early 19th century, the roughly circular shape of the park was enhanced by the fine terraces and two circular roads within the park designed by John Nash under the patronage of the Prince Regent, later George IV. The park has an athletics track, tennis courts, cricket, rounders, baseball and football pitches. The Inner Circle contains Queen Mary's Gardens with a rose garden. There is a boating lake (Boat hire March-October Tel: 01-486 4759/7905). Military band concerts during summer. Open air theatre (01-935 5756). To the north is London Zoo (see separate entry) and during the summer, a waterbus service by canal links the zoo with Little Venice in Maida Vale and Camden Lock See p. 36).

SPORTS CENTRES

Fitness Centre (L)
11 Floral Street, WC2
Tel: 01-836 6544
🚇 Covent Garden

Adjoining the Sanctuary, the Fitness Centre has a Nautilus gym, sauna, jacuzzi, beauty treatments, a hairdressing salon, shop and health bar.

Jubilee Hall Recreation Centre
Central Market Square, Covent Garden, WC2
Tel: 01-836 4835
🚇 Covent Garden

*Facilities currently housed in the basement area include weight-training, dance and exercise classes, yoga and sunbeds.
From May 1987, the Sports Centre will occupy the first floors of the Jubilee Hall and adjacent building and many more facilities will be available including indoor sports halls and sauna.*

Marshall Street Centre
Marshall Street, Soho, W1
Tel: 01-798 2007
🚇 Oxford Circus

2 swimming pools (larger pool under repair), multi-gym, martial arts centre. (Squash courts under construction – phone for details.)

Paddington Recreation Ground
Randolph Avenue, Paddington, W9
Tel: 01-798 3642
🚇 Maida Vale

Outdoor sports centre with athletics and cycling tracks, 3 football pitches, bowling and netball pitches and "free-play" area.

Porchester Centre
Queensway, Bayswater, W2
Tel: 01-798 3689
🚇 Bayswater

Fitness room, swimming pool, Turkish and Russian Baths.

Queen Mother's Sport Centre
223 Vauxhall Bridge Road, SW1
Tel: 01-798 2125 (enquiries) 01-834 4726 (bookings)
🚇 Victoria

Sports hall, squash, multi-gym, exercise facilities and swimming pool.

Sanctuary (L)
11 Floral Street, WC2
Tel: 01-240 9635/6
🚇 Covent Garden

Tropical watergarden, swimming pool, sauna, sunbeds, beauty treatments and health bar. There is also a Natural Therapy Centre (Tel: 01-379 6858) FOR LADIES ONLY.

Westbourne Green Sports Complex
Torquay Street, Paddington, W2
Tel: 01-798 3707
🚇 Royal Oak

Outdoor sports centre offers facilities for football, tennis, cricket, basket and netball, and rollerskating.

THEATRES

Major London theatres (alphabetical, not by borough)

Adelphi
Strand, WC2
Box Office: 01-836 7611/240 7913-4
Credit Cards: 01-836 7358
⊖ Charing Cross

Albery
St. Martin's Lane, WC2
Box Office: 01-836 3878
Credit Cards: 01-379 6565
⊖ Leicester Square

Aldwych
Aldwych, WC2
Box Office: 01-836 6404/0641
Credit Cards: 01-379 6233/741 9999
⊖ Holborn

Ambassadors
West Street, Cambridge Circus, WC2
Box Office: 01-836 6111
Credit Cards: 01-836 1171
⊖ Leicester Square

Apollo
Shaftesbury Avenue, W1
Box Office: 01-437 2663
Credit Cards: 01-434 3598
⊖ Piccadilly Circus

Apollo Victoria
17 Wilton Road, SW1
Box Office: 01-828 8665
Credit Cards: 01-630 6262
⊖ Victoria

Barbican
Barbican Centre, EC2
Box Office: 01-628 8795/638 8891
(& Credit Cards)
⊖ Barbican (closed Sundays)/Moorgate

Coliseum
St. Martin's Lane, WC2
Box Office: 01-836 3161
Credit Cards: 01-240 5258
⊖ Leicester Square/Charing Cross

Comedy
Panton Street, SW1
Box Office: 01-930 2578
⊖ Piccadilly Circus

Covent Garden Royal Opera House, WC2
Box Office: 01-240 1066
Credit Cards: 01-240 1911
⊖ Covent Garden

Criterion
Piccadilly Circus, W1
Box Office: 01-930 3216
Credit Cards: 01-379 6565
⊖ Piccadilly Circus

Donmar Warehouse
Earlham Street, Covent Garden, WC2
Box Office: 01-240 8230
Credit Cards: 01-379 6565
⊖ Covent Garden

Drury Lane
Theatre Royal, Catherine Street, WC2
Box Office: 01-836 8108/240 9066-7 (& CC)
⊖ Covent Garden

THEATRES

Duchess
Catherine Street, WC2
Box Office: 01-836 8243/240 9648
🚇 Covent Garden

Duke of York's
St. Martin's Lane, WC2
Box Office: 01-836 5122
Credit Cards: 01-836 9837
🚇 Leicester Square

Fortune
Russell Street, WC2
Box Office and Credit Cards: 01-836 2238
🚇 Covent Garden

Garrick
Charing Cross Road, WC2
Box Office and Credit Cards: 01-379 6107
🚇 Leicester Square

Globe
Shaftesbury Avenue, W1
Box Office: 01-437 1592
Credit Cards: 01-741 9999
🚇 Piccadilly Circus

Haymarket
Theatre Royal, Haymarket, SW1
Box Office and Credit Cards: 01-930 9832
🚇 Piccadilly Circus

Her Majesty's
Haymarket, SW1
Box Office: 01-839 2244
🚇 Piccadilly Circus

Lyric
Shaftesbury Avenue, W1
Box Office: 01-437 3686/434 1050
Credit Cards: 01-434 1050/734 5166/7
🚇 Piccadilly Circus

Mayfair
Stratton Street, W1
Box Office and Credit Cards: 01-629 3036
🚇 Green Park

Mermaid
Puddledock, Blackfriars, EC4
Box Office and Credit Cards: 01-236 5568
🚇 Blackfriars

National Theatre
South Bank, SE1
Box Office and Credit Cards: 01-928 2252
🚇 Waterloo

New London
Drury Lane, WC2
Box Office: 01-405 0072
Credit Cards: 01-404 4079
🚇 Covent Garden/Holborn

Old Vic
Waterloo Road, SE1
Box Office: 01-928 7616
Credit Cards: 01-261 1821
🚇 Waterloo

Palace
Shaftesbury Avenue, W1
Box Office: 01-434 0909
🚇 Leicester Square

continued overleaf

THEATRES

Palladium
Argyll Street, W1
Box Office: 01-437 7373/2055
Credit Cards: 01-734 8961
⊖ Oxford Circus

Phoenix
Charing Cross Road, WC2
Box Office: 01-836 2294
Credit Cards: 01-240 9661
⊖ Tottenham Court Road/Leicester Square

Piccadilly
Denman Street, W1
Box Office: 01-437 4506
Credit Cards: 01-379 6565/379 6433
⊖ Piccadilly Circus

Prince Edward
Old Compton Street, W1
Box Office: 01-734 8951
⊖ Leicester Square

Prince of Wales
Coventry Street, W1
Box Office: 01-930 8681/2
Credit Cards: 01-930 0844/5/6
⊖ Piccadilly Circus

Queens
Shaftesbury Avenue, W1
Box Office: 01-734 1166-7 0261/0120/439 3849/4031
⊖ Piccadilly Circus

Royal Court
Sloane Square, SW1
Box Office and Credit Cards: 01-730 1745/1857
⊖ Sloane Square

Sadler's Wells
Roseberry Avenue, EC1
Box Office and Credit Cards: 01-278 8916
⊖ Angel

Savoy
Strand, WC2
Box Office: 01-836 8888
Credit Cards: 01-379 6219/836 0479
⊖ Charing Cross

Shaftesbury Theatre of Comedy
Shaftesbury Avenue, WC2
Box Office: 01-379 5399
⊖ Tottenham Court Road

St. Martin's
West Street, Cambridge Circus, WC2
Box Office and Credit Cards: 01-836 1443
⊖ Leicester Square

Strand
Aldwych, WC2
Box Office: 01-836 2660
Credit Cards: 01-836 5190/4143
⊖ Charing Cross

Vaudeville
Strand, WC2
Box Office: 01-836 9987/5645
⊖ Charing Cross

Victoria Palace
Victoria Street, SW1
Box Office and Credit Cards: 01-834 1317/828 4735
⊖ Victoria

Westminster
Palace Street, SW1
Box Office: 01-834 0283-4
Credit Cards: 01-834 0048
⊖ Victoria

Whitehall
Whitehall, SW1
Box Office: 01-930 7765/839 4455
Credit Cards: 01-379 6565
⊖ Charing Cross

Wyndham's
Charing Cross Road, WC2
Box Office: 01-836 3028
Credit Cards: 01-379 6565
⊖ Leicester Square

THEATRE TICKETS

Half Price Ticket Booth
Leicester Square, WC2
Theatre tickets are available at half the normal price (plus service fee) to personal callers on a cash only basis.
Open: Mon-Sat 1430-1830 (Matinee days additional 1200-1400)
⊖ Leicester Square

LAMBETH

The London Borough of Lambeth borders the Boroughs of Southwark to the east and Wandsworth to the west; it stretches from the River Thames in the north to Streatham in the south. The suburban areas of Brixton, Clapham, Kennington and Streatham are covered in detail in LVCB's *Exploring Outer London* guide (see page 64).

The Archbishop of Canterbury's official residence at Lambeth Palace dates from 1495. It is not open to the public, but it is planned to open the gardens within the next two years.

Major attractions include the South Bank Arts Complex, situated on the south bank of the river. The Festival of Britain in 1951 was the inspiration for this complex which includes the Royal Festival Hall, two further concert halls and the Hayward Gallery and National Film Theatre. Since 1976, the National Theatre Company, founded by Laurence Olivier at the nearby Old Vic Theatre, has been part of the South Bank.

Also on the South Bank are the Jubilee Gardens, designed for the Queen's Silver Jubilee in 1977. Beside the Gardens lies County Hall, built in 1912 to accommodate the former Greater London Council. Plans for its future are not known but it still houses the Inner London Education Authority.

For further information on the borough contact: Lambeth Town Hall, Brixton Hill SW2 1RW. Tel: 01-274 7722. Open: Mon-Fri 0930-1700. (Information)

continued overleaf

PLACES OF INTEREST

ART GALLERIES

Hayward Gallery (L)
South Bank, Belvedere Road, SE1
Tel: 01-928 3144. Recorded information on 01-261 0127
Open: Mon-Wed 1000-2000, Thu-Sat 1000-1800, Sun 1200-1800; closed between exhibitions
Admission: Charge
✪ Waterloo

The concrete building forms part of the South Bank complex and houses mainly modern exhibitions on two levels. Small bookshop.

MUSEUMS

Museum of Garden History (L)
St. Mary at Lambeth, Lambeth Palace Road, SE1
Tel: 01-261 1891
Open: Mon-Fri 1100-1500, Sun 1030-1700 (closed Dec-March)
Admission: Free
✪ Westminster. Bus 77, 159, 170 or 507 from Victoria

17th century botanical garden with many period and rare plants introduced into the country by the Tradescants father and son. John Tradescant (the father) was Charles I's gardener. The church is owned by the Tradescant Trust. It retains its 14th century tower and was restored in 1851-2. Three generations of Tradescants, as well as William Bligh (1817) of Mutiny of the 'Bounty' are buried in the churchyard.

ENTERTAINMENT

The South Bank Complex
Belvedere Road, SE1
Open: 1000-2300
✪ Waterloo Embankment

Development of the South Bank site started for the Festival of Britain in 1951 which took place here. The area now includes three concert halls, the Hayward Art Gallery (see separate entry), the National Theatre, the National Film Theatre, a crafts centre, bars and restaurants. Plans for improving the area includes removing the walkways. Since 1986 the South Bank Board has been responsible for most of the area (but not the National Theatre and the National Film Theatre).

South Bank Concert Halls
Tel: 01-928 3002 General Information
Tel: 01-928 3191 To reserve tickets
♿ Access

Royal Festival Hall – *the main concert hall seats 3000. There are guided tours of the concert hall, including backstage, at 1245 and 1730.*
Queen Elizabeth Hall – *(opened 1967) seats 1100.*
Purcell Room – *seats 330.*
(Regular free concerts and exhibitions take place in the foyer areas (1000-2200) and Lyre Room (RFH) and there are several eating areas.)

National Theatre (L)
Tel: 01-928 8126 Recorded Booking Information
Tel: 01-928 2252 For Bookings (Box Office 1000-2000 Mon-Sat)
Tel: 01-633 0880 Other Information (1000-2300 daily)
♿ Access

Opened in 1976; the repertoire system enables the National Theatre to offer audiences the choice of at least six different productions at any one time. Tours of the building, including backstage, Mon-Sat: 1015, 1230, 1245, 1730 and 1800 (except on Olivier matinee days: 1015, 1245 and 1745). Tel: 01-633 0880 (Lyttelton information desk) to book. There are bookshops, a restaurant and bars and buffets. Exhibitions and free entertainment in the foyer.
The Olivier – *fan shaped auditorium, largest of the three theatres, seats over 1000.*
Lyttelton – *adaptable proscenium theatre.*
Cottesloe – *smallest of the three theatres.*

Old Vic Theatre (L)
The Cut, Waterloo Road, SE1
Tel: 01-928 7616
✪ Waterloo

Built in 1817, it became one of London's leading theatres under the management of Lillian Baylis from 1912. From 1963 it was the home of the National Theatre before the company transferred to the South Bank. The Old Vic is now owned by Canadian millionaire Ed Mirvish, who spent £1m on its restoration in 1980-83.

National Film Theatre
Tel: 01-928 3232
♿ Access

The British Film Institute opened the NFT on this site under Waterloo Bridge in 1958. The four auditoria show a changing programme of arts and popular films. Cafeteria. Bookshop. Daily and weekly membership available.

PARKS AND OPEN SPACES

Archbishops Park
⊖ Lambeth North

The 20 acre park was opened to the public in 1901, formed out of part of the grounds of Lambeth Palace. It is mostly grassland with trees and shrubs and has a children's playground and a putting green (May-Sept). The adjoining Palace grounds are due to open to the public in 1988.

Jubilee Gardens
⊖ Waterloo

The gardens between the South Bank Complex and County Hall designed for the Queen's Silver Jubilee in 1977.

SHOPPING

South Bank Crafts Centre
Open: 1100-1900 Tues-Sun
⊖ Waterloo

Situated in the Hungerford Arches next to the Royal Festival Hall, it features the work of new artists for sale at reasonable prices. The craftspersons can also be seen at work.

MARKETS

Lower Marsh
Lambeth, SE1
Open: Mon-Fri 1000-1500
(Sat bric-a-brac market to open shortly 0900-1700)
Best times: Lunchtime
⊖ Waterloo
Fruit; clothes; vegetables.

LAMBETH

CAMDEN

The London Borough of Camden lies to the north-east of London adjoining the City and the West-End in the south, stretching out to Hampstead and Highgate in the north. It is composed of the former Boroughs of Holborn, Hampstead and St. Pancras. Attractions in the north of the borough are covered in detail in LVCB's *Exploring Outer London* guide. This guide concentrates on the attractions south of Euston Road.

Throughout the Middle Ages, the Bishop of Chichester owned land to the west of Chancery Lane which was leased to the Society of Lincoln's Inn. It is the oldest of the four Inns of Court in London and dates from 1422. The Inns of Court still have the exclusive right to call persons to the Bar; they provide training for law students and acccommodation for practising barristers and solicitors.

In the 14th century, the Blemonde family held land in the area from which the name Bloomsbury is derived. By 1660, the Earl of Southampton had acquired the manor of Bloomsbury and built a mansion with a square in front of it, now called Bloomsbury Square. Among the fine buildings was Montagu House, on the site of the present British Museum (begun in 1753). The landowning families of the Russells, Dukes of Bedford, have given their names to many of the squares which are characteristic of the area: Russell, Tavistock, Bedford, Woburn.

British Museum, Camden

Bloomsbury's intellectual reputation was enhanced with the establishment of University College in 1827. Bloomsbury became fashionable with writers, painters, musicians and also lawyers, who found it convenient for Lincoln's Inn and Gray's Inn and it enjoyed a "Bohemian" reputation before the First World War through Virginia Woolf and Lytton Strachey who were part of the "Bloomsbury Group".

Today, the British Musuem, the University of London and its many colleges, together with several major hospitals, dominate the area.

Until the end of the 18th century, Camden was a quiet country area; it was not until the 1820's that the building of the Regent's Canal brought small industry. The furnishing trade prospered, centred along Tottenham Court Road. Now replaced by offices, the long-established furniture store Heal's is a reminder of that era. Today, the road is better known for its many hi-fi and camera stores; to the west there are still fashion workshops and showrooms and the offices of Independent Television News in the shadow of British Telecom Tower, 580 feet high and completed in 1964 (closed to the public).

Camden is a lively and diverse borough with over one hundred acres of parks and gardens; in the southern part, there are six West-End theatres and an abundance of cinemas. The London Contempory Dance Theatre is based at the Place Theatre in Dukes Road (Tel: 01-387 0031). A major event in the borough is the annual Camden Arts Festival of Dance, Music, Opera and Jazz, held at various venues in early Spring, including the Bloomsbury Theatre (01-388 3363) and Drill Hall (01-637 8270).

For further information on Camden contact: Camden Information Service, Town Hall Extension, Euston Road, WC1 2RU. Tel: 01-278 4444 ext. 2165/2764. Mon-Fri 0900-1700, (Thurs 0900-1800).

PLACES OF INTEREST

ART GALLERIES

Courtauld Institute Galleries
Woburn Square, WC1
Tel: 01-580 1015
Open: Mon-Sat 1000-1700, Sun 1400-1700; closed Christmas, Easter, and Bank Holidays
Admission: Charge
⊖ Goodge Street/Russell Square

The gallery is on the 4th floor of a university building and contains the Princes Gate Collection of Old Master paintings and drawings and the Courtauld Collection of Impressionists and Post Impressionists, one of the finest collections outside France. Among the works on view are Manet's "A Bar at the Folies Bergere" and Renoir's "La Loge", but only a portion of the collections can be shown here. A move to Somerset House is planned in the next two years. Bookshop.

continued overleaf

CAMDEN

Percival David Foundation of Chinese Art
53 Gordon Square, WC1
Tel: 01-387 3909
Open: Mon 1400-1700, Tue-Fri 1030-1700 (closed 1300-1400), Sat 1030-1300; closed on Bank Holidays and on preceding Saturdays, Saturdays during August
Admission: Free
⊖ Euston Square

Three galleries of outstanding Chinese ceramics from the tenth to the 19th centuries, collected and bequeathed by Sir Percival David, former governor of the School of Oriental and African Studies.

Photographers' Gallery (L)
5 & 8 Great Newport Street, WC2
Tel: 01-240 5511
Open: Tue-Sat 1100-1900
♿ Access
Admission: Free
⊖ Leicester Square

Regular exhibition of photography on different subjects. Reference library contains 1,500 books and 10,000 slides.

Thomas Coram Foundation for Children
40 Brunswick Square, WC1
Tel: 01-278 2424
Open: Mon-Fri 1000-1600; Closed Public holidays and when rooms in use for conferences
Admission: Charge
⊖ Russell Square

The galleries contain about 120 paintings and etchings including works by Hogarth, Gainsborough and Kneller, musical scores by Handel as well as mementos of the old Foundling Hospital founded in 1739 by a kindly Sea-Captain, Thomas Coram to care for abandoned children.

MUSEUMS

British Library
Great Russell Street, WC1
Tel: 01-636 1544
Open: Mon-Sat 1000-1700, Sun 1430-1800; Closed Christmas, New Year's Day, Good Friday, Tours of Reading Room on the hour between 1100 to 1600 weekdays
Admission: Free
♿ Access
⊖ Tottenham Court Road/Russell Square

*The British Library collection of some 8m books is housed within the British Museum. The famous Reading Room with its 100ft high dome is only accessible to ticket holders or on regular tours. The galleries show some of the collection including the Magna Carta, Shakespeare's works and many famous author's manuscripts as well as royal signatures and a copy of Marx's "Das Kapital", written here. Changing exhibitions.
The British Library is due to move to a new building near King's Cross in the early 1990s. Bookshop.*

British Museum
Great Russell Street, WC1
Tel: 01-636 1555
Open: Mon-Sat 1000-1700, Sun 1430-1800; Closed Christmas, New Year's Day, Good Friday
Admission: Free
♿ Access
⊖ Tottenham Court Road/Russell Square

The British Museum dates from 1753; the present, main building dates from 1823 and the 1840s. It contains a huge collection of Greek and Roman antiquities including the Elgin Marbles; Egyptian treasures including the Rosetta Stone, tombs and mummies; British antiquities include the Mildenhall and Sutton Hoo treasures – Roman silverware and the content of a 7th century ship burial from Suffolk. Cafeteria. Bookshop. Tours and lectures.

Marble Cargatio, British Museum

CAMDEN

Dickens House and Museum
48 Doughty Street, WC1
Tel: 01-405 2127

Open: Mon-Sat 0930-1700; closed Bank Holidays and Sunday
Admission: Charge
⊖ Russell Square

Dickens lived here from 1837-39, during which time he worked on three novels; "The Pickwick Papers", "Nicholas Nickleby" and "Oliver Twist". The house contains Dickens' desk and chair, his drawing room, paintings, letters and the Dickens Library, one of the most comprehensive in the world. Shop.

Jewish Museum
Woburn House, Upper Woburn Place, WC1
Tel: 01-388 4525

Open: Tues-Thurs (Fri during Summer) 1000-1600; Sun (and Friday during Winter) 1000-1245; Closed Sat, Mon, Public, and Jewish Holidays.
Admission: Free
⊖ Euston/Euston Square/Russell Square

The museum contains a collection of ritual objects and antiquities illustrating Jewish life and worship including Scrolls of the Law, the Shofar Rams' Horns and a 16th-century Venetian Ark. Audio-visual programmes explain the Jewish faith and customs.

Public Records Office Library and Museum
Chancery Lane, WC2
Tel: 01-405 0741

Open: Library open for research 0930-1700 Mon-Fri. Entry by Readers Ticket, (issued on production of proof of identification). Museum closed, until autumn 1987.
⊖ Chancery Lane

The museum recently staged the "Domesday" exhibition, in celebration of the nine hundredth anniversary of the compilation of the "Domesday Book". It is now due to reopen to the public in Autumn 1987.

Sir John Soane's Museum
13 Lincoln's Inn Fields, WC2
Tel: 01-405 2107

Open: Tue-Sat 1000-1700; Closed Bank Holidays. (Architectural Library 1000-1300, 1400-1700 by appointment)
Admission: Free
⊖ Holborn

This former residence of Sir John Soane, the architect of the Bank of England and other buildings, contains over 20,000 architectural drawings, antiquities and works by Hogarth, Turner, Watteau.

Petrie Museum of Egyptian Archaeology
University College London, Gower Street, WC1
Tel: 01-387 7050 ex 617

Open: Mon-Fri 1000-1200 & 1315-1700; Closed Bank Holidays, 1 week over Christmas & Easter & up to 4 weeks in Summer (check before visit)
Admission: Free
⊖ Warren Street/Euston Square

A university teaching collection open to the public, assembled by British Archaeologist Sir Flinders Petrie. Includes archaeological material from Prehistoric to Coptic periods in Egyptian history. Closed for renovation until late 1987.

Elong statue of a negress, Petrie Museum

HISTORIC BUILDINGS

Old Curiosity Shop
13-14 Portsmouth Street, WC2
Tel: 01-405 9891

Open: 0900-1730 Mon-Fri, 0900-1700 Sat & Sun (April-Oct), 0930-1700 Mon-Fri, 0930-1700 Sat & Sun (Nov-March)
♿ Access
⊖ Holborn

The building dates from 1567 with two staircases and an original fireplace upstairs. It contains items owned by Dickens and is, many believe, the home of Dickens' heroine in "Little Nell". Today the shop sells gifts and antiques.

continued overleaf

35

CAMDEN

Gray's Inn, WC2
Tel: 01-405 8164
Open: 1200-1430 Mon-Fri Gardens only, (Chapel and Hall open by appointment only)
⊖ Chancery Lane

Some buildings of this Inn of Court date to the 16th century but were heavily restored after Second World War damage. Gardens laid out by Sir Francis Bacon in 1606. A Chapel has stood on the same site since 1315.

Lincoln's Inn, WC2
Tel: 01-405 1393
Open: Mon-Fri 1200-1430
Admission: Free
⊖ Holborn

Lincoln's Inn was founded in the 14th century for students of the law and barristers. The Lincoln's Inn Chapel was begun in 1619 with an open undercroft where the students could "confer for their learning" and where legal practitioners met their clients. Old Hall dates from 1492; New Hall and Library from 1845. New Square, garden and chapel open to the public. Halls can be seen by appointment only.

Staple Inn
High Holborn, WC1
⊖ Holborn

Originally a hostel for wool-staplers, hence the name, Staple Inn became an Inn of Chancery from Henry V's reign until the late 19th century. Its function then was to train and house the Mediaeval Chancery Clerks and later it trained students of law wishing to be called to the Bar by the Inns of Court. The Staple Hall is not open to the public but the timbered façade is particularly worth noting as it is a survivor of the Great Fire and dates from 1586.

OTHER PLACES OF INTEREST

London Zoo (L)
Regent's Park, NW1
Tel: 01-722 3333
Open: 1 Mar-31 Oct, 0900-1800 (or dusk, whichever is earlier), 1900 on Sun & Bank Holidays; Nov-Feb, 1000-dusk
Admission: Charge
♿ Access
⊖ Camden Town

The Zoological Gardens were established in 1825; and the public was first admitted from 1847. More than 8,000 animals are on view and a comprehensive programme of redevelopment is under way to improve the areas for each group of animals. Educational programmes, tours, special events. Restaurant, Cafeteria.
Through the northern edge of Regent's Park (see separate entry) runs the Regent's Canal which first opened in 1820. A waterbus service operates along a stretch of the canal between Little Venice in Maida Vale (⊖ Warwick Avenue) and Camden Lock (⊖ Camden Town/Chalk Farm), passing through London Zoo. The London Waterbus Company (Tel: 01-482 2550) operates this service and offers reduced entry price tickets for the Zoo combined with the canal trip. Daily March-early October and on weekends and holidays October-Easter.

CHURCHES

St. Etheldreda's
Ely Place, WC2

Britains oldest Catholic church dating from 13th century rebuilt in 1874. This was the chapel for the Bishop of Ely's residence.

St. Giles In the Fields
High Holborn, WC2

A leper hospital was founded here in the 12th century with its own church; rebuilt in 1731 by Henry Flitcroft. Interesting monuments.

St. Pancras Old Church
Pancras Road, NW1
⊖ Kings Cross St. Pancras

Dedicated to St. Pancras, patron of youth, St. Pancras Old Church was probably founded in the 12th century. It contains an Altar-Stone said to date from the 6th century and a monument to the architect Sir John Soane (see Sir John Soane Museum, separate entry). The poet Shelley first met and fell in love with Mary Godwin in the churchyard when she went to visit her mother's grave.

SPORT
Cycling
Somers Town Cycle Route
A special route has been designed for cyclists between Camden Town and Bloomsbury, mainly along quiet residential roads. Special crossings have been provided where the route meets the busy intersections at Crowndale Road and Euston Road. A free map of the route is available from Camden Town Hall extension in Argyle Street off Euston Road, or ring Camden's Planning and Communications office Tel: 01-278 4444 Ext. 2847.

Sports Centres
Oasis Sports Centre
32 Endell Street, WC2
Tel: 01-836 9555/01-831 1804 for reservations
⊖ Covent Garden/Tottenham Court Road/Holborn
Facilities include heated indoor and outdoor swimming pools, sports hall, multi-gym, sauna and dance and exercise classes.

OPEN SPACES/PARKS
Coram Fields, WC1
Open: Mon-Fri 0830-2000 (open till 1630 in Winter), Sat & Sun 0900-2000 (open till 1630 in Winter).
Childrens playground.

Lincolns Inn Fields, WC1
Planned by Inigo Jones in the early 17th century, this is the largest of all the central London squares and contains trees, gardens and playing fields. There are tennis courts for hire (Tel: 01-405 5194 for bookings) and netball courts (Tel: 01-435 7171 Ext. 14 for bookings).

Grays Inn Fields, WC1
Open: Mon-Fri 1200-1430 (May-Sept only) (see above)
One of the loveliest gardens of all the Inns of Court.

SHOPPING
Major shops and stores are to be found along Tottenham Court Road (⊖ Tottenham Court Road) including specialists in Hi-Fi and photographic equipment. Many jewellers shops are based in Hatton Garden (⊖ Chancery Lane). The Brunswick Centre (⊖ Russell Square) houses a supermarket, restaurants, a fitness and health centre and the Renoir cinema.

MARKETS
Leather Lane, EC1
Open: Mon-Fri 1000-1430. Best times: Lunch time
⊖ Chancery Lane
Household goods; clothes.

London Silver Vaults
Chancery Lane, WC2
Open: Mon-Fri 0900-1730, Sat 0900-1230
⊖ Chancery Lane
Antique and modern silver, jewellery are for sale in these vaults below ground level.

CITY

⊖ Bank (Central & Northern lines)

The City is the ancient heart of London. Founded in Roman times along the river Thames, Londonium quickly became a major commercial and administrative centre. A stone wall was built around the City in AD 200, which determined the shape of London for more than one thousand years. Some sections of it can still be seen today in the sunken garden at St. Alphage just off London Wall, and nearby at the Museum of London, as well as outside Tower Hill underground station. You can follow the Roman wall with the help of a map from the Museum of London and plaques at regular intervals. Within the "Square Mile", the City still thrives as one of the world's foremost financial and business centre, an area rich in tradition and historic buildings despite the disasters that have befallen it. An outbreak of the Plague occured in 1665, followed by the Great Fire of London in 1666 when three fifths of the City was destroyed. In this century, one third of the City was destroyed in the Blitz bombing raids of the Second World War.

Some of the City's major institutions originated in the Coffee Houses that abounded towards the end of the 17th century. Each Coffee House attracted a clientele of people of similar interests: Financiers began to frequent "Jonathan's" in Exchange Alley and merchants who wanted news of shipping went to "Edward Lloyd's" in Lombard Street, which grew into "Lloyd's of London", the International Insurance Market in Lime Street. Lloyd's is now established in a striking new building. The public can observe, for the first time, the trading activities of the market from a special viewing gallery.

Other major institutions include the Bank of England, founded in 1694, and affectionately known as "The Old Lady of Threadneedle Street", now occupying a building completed in 1939; and the Stock Exchange in Old Broad Street founded in 1801 which plays a key role in Britain's economy. It is also housed in a modern building with a public viewing gallery overlooking the trading floor. The relative newcomer, the London International Financial Futures Exchange, is housed in the Royal Exchange building.

Since the 11th century there has been a prison where the Central Criminal Court now stands. The notorious Newgate prison, described in three of Charles Dickens' books, was demolished in 1902 to make way for this building more commonly known as "The Old Bailey". It has jurisdiction over

Greater London and many famous cases have been tried in its number one court. It is possible to attend trials when the courts are sitting.

Civil law in action can be observed at the imposing Law Court in the Strand – they are the Royal Courts of Justice established on this site since 1874.

No picture of the City is complete without St. Paul's Cathedral, Sir Christopher Wren's masterpiece, scene of the wedding of the Prince and Princess of Wales in 1981 and many other state occasions. In addition there are some forty-four churches, many designed by Wren, within the City.

Fleet Street has long been associated with printing and publishing. It was an apprentice of the printer William Caxton who brought the first printing press to Fleet Street in the 15th century, so attracting writers and poets to the area. But the introduction of new technology has led major newspapers to look for new sites in Docklands and elsewhere, and Fleet Street will not be synonomous with newspapers for much longer.

Many City institutions and businesses are also looking east to expand. The London Docklands Light Railway, due to be completed in July 1987, will link the City with the Isle of Dogs and Stratford East with stations at Bank and Tower Hill (The Minories).

The growing number of merchants and craftsmen in London soon organised themselves into various Craft Guilds as early as the 12th century to protect their interests. They became the Livery Companies of which there are now over ninety, a number of which have their own magnificent halls in the City. The Liverymen play a vital part in the

The Lord Mayor's Coach

continued overleaf

government of the City and in the election of the Lord Mayor of London; the Court of Common Council – the elected authority – meets in the Guildhall, which dates to the 15th century.

One of the major events of the year is the Lord Mayor's Show, held on the second Saturday in November. It is a long procession taking the newly-elected Lord Mayor to make his Declaration of Office before the Lord Chief Justice at the Royal Courts of Justice in the Strand. Until 1856, this colourful pageant was held on the Thames, but now the Lord Mayor travels from Mansion House, the traditional residence, in a magnificent gilded coach, in a procession which also includes military bands and floats decorated along a theme suggested by the new Lord Mayor.

More details of the traditions and history of the City of London can be found in LVCB's booklet, *Traditional London*, see page 64.

The Barbican occupies a site that was heavily bombed during the war and takes its name from the ancient outer fortifications of the City. The Barbican Centre was opened in 1982 and includes one of the largest art galleries in London as well as restaurants, three cinemas, two theatres and a concert hall. It is the home of the Royal Shakespeare Company and also the London Symphony Orchestra. Adjoining the Centre is a vast housing complex, a school and an ancient church, St. Giles Cripplegate. The City of London Festival is held in July and features classical and jazz music, poetry recitals and cabaret performances in many of the City's livery halls and churches.

For further information on the square mile of the City of London contact: City of London Information Centre, St. Paul's Churchyard, EC4. Tel: 01-606 3030 ask for Information Centre. Open: Mon-Fri 0930-1700, Sat 0930-1300, (Nov-March Sat 0930-1230).

PLACES OF INTEREST

ART GALLERIES

Barbican Art Gallery
Barbican Centre, Silk Street, Barbican, EC2
Tel: 01-638 4141
Open: Tue-Sat 1000-1845, Sun 1200-1745
Admission: Charge (varies depending on exhibition)
Access
Barbican (closed Sundays)/Moorgate
Part of the Barbican Centre for Arts and Conferences, it has changing temporary exhibitions.

MUSEUMS

Guildhall Clock Museum
Guildhall, Aldermanbury, EC2
Tel: 01-606 3030
Open: 0930-1645 Mon-Fri
Admission: Free
Access
Bank/Mansion House
The collection of clocks and watches, dating from the 1600s was bequeathed to the museum by the Clockmakers Company. It is one of the most important collections in the country.

CITY

Great Fire of London

Museum of London
London Wall, EC2
Tel: 01-600 3699
Open: Tue-Sat 1000-1800, Sun 1400-1800; Closed every Mon (inc Bank Holidays)
Admission: Free
♿ Access
⊖ St. Paul's/Barbican/Moorgate

London's history illustrated chronologically from prehistory to the present day. Domestic and ceremonial life is shown including the Lord Mayor's State Coach of 1757 and still used in the Lord Mayor's Show in November. Remains of the London Wall, built by the Romans and a mediaeval tower can be seen nearby in the gardens on the east side of the museum. Many archaeological finds are shown, some quite recently discovered. It is possible to walk along the route of the Roman Wall from the Museum to the Tower of London, using the special map. Lectures, films, tours, special exhibitions, cafeteria.

National Postal Museum
King Edward Building, King Edward Street, EC1
Tel: 01-432 3851
Open: Mon-Thur 0930-1630, Fri 0930-1600; Closed first week in October and Bank Holidays
Admission: Free
⊖ St. Paul's

Contains one of the most important and extensive collections of postage stamps in the world, including the Phillips and Berne Collections.

Telecom Technology Showcase
135 Queen Victoria Street, EC4
Tel: 01-248 7444
Open: Mon-Fri 1000-1700; Closed Bank Holidays
Admission: Free
♿ Access
⊖ Blackfriars

The Showcase presents a complete history of telecommunications in Britain and looks forward to the future. Souvenir and bookshop.

HISTORIC BUILDINGS/HOUSES

Central Criminal Court
Old Bailey, EC4
Tel: 01-248 3277
Open: Public Galleries only: Mon-Fri 1015-1300 & 1350-1600; Closed on Bank Holidays. Children under 14 not admitted.
Admission: Free
⊖ St. Paul's

The site of Old Newgate Prison, now London's major criminal court.

Dr. Johnson's House
17 Gough Square, EC4
Tel: 01-353 3745
Open: Oct-April, Mon-Sat 1100-1700; May-Sept, Mon-Sat 1100-1730; Closed Bank Holidays
Admission: Charge
⊖ Blackfriars/Temple

Dr. Johnson compiled his famous dictionary

continued overleaf

41

CITY

in the attic of this 17th century house, his home from 1749-58. Among the relics on show is an early edition of the dictionary and portraits of Dr. Johnson and his friends, including a painting of James Boswell by Sir Joshua Reynolds.

Guildhall
Gresham Street, EC2
Tel: 01-606 3030

Open: Mon-Sat 1000-1700, Sun (May-Sept), Spring/Autumn Bank Holiday, 1000-1700; Closed Christmas Day, Boxing Day, Good Friday, Easter Monday, New Year's Day
Admission: Free

⊖ Bank/St. Paul's/Mansion House

The court of Common Council meets in the Great Hall every third Thursday and the public is admitted.

The centre of civic government for the square mile of the City of London, dates from 1411. On view in the Great Hall is a 15th century window, monuments to important national figures including Admiral Nelson, the Duke of Wellington and Churchill. Also nine feet high statues of the legendary giants, Gog and Magog who represent the conflict between the ancient inhabitants of Britain and Trojan invaders. The crypts can also be visited. The Guildhall Library was founded in 1425 and includes some valuable historic documents on London.

LIVERY HALLS

The Livery Companies in the City of London were founded in the Middle Ages. Some companies including the Apothecaries and Goldsmiths still exert great authority over their trade or craft. In spite of extensive damage in the last war, many of the Livery Companies boast magnificent Halls. A large number had to be rebuilt after the war although some of the ancient features remain. These may be visited at certain times during the year. A list of the Livery Company's "Open Days" and details of bookings is available from March from the City of London Information Centre. Tel: 01-606 3030 and ask for the Information Centre.

Here is a small selection of some of the more interesting Halls:

Drapers Hall
Throgmorton Avenue, EC2
Tel: 01-588 5001

This is the third oldest Hall in the City. It was built after the Great Fire and restored in 1949.

Official robes of the Lord Mayor of London

Fishmongers Hall
London Bridge, EC4
Tel: 01-626 3531

The Fishmongers Company, the fourth oldest of the livery companies, still carries out its ancient duties such as examining all fish coming into Billingsgate Market on the Isle of Dogs. Treasures include Annigoni's portrait of the Queen. The hall dates from 1830 with later restorations.

Goldsmith's Hall
Foster Lane, EC2
Tel: 01-606 8971 Ext. 208

The fifth oldest livery company. The present Hall dates from 1835 and contains magnificent displays of gold and silver. The Goldsmith's Company still stamps gold and silverplate.

Haberdashers Hall
Staining Street, EC2
Tel: 01-606-0967

Rebuilt after Second World War, the present Hall contains paintings by famous artists including Sir Joshua Reynolds.

Vintners Hall
Upper Thames Street, EC4
Tel: 01-236 1863

Contains tapestries and paintings. The Vintners Company is entitled to own swans – only the Dyers' Company and the Queen can also own swans on the Thames, see details of Swan Upping, the annual marking of swans, in Traditional London (see p. 60).

CITY

Mansion House
Mansion House Street, EC4
Tel: 01-626 2500

Open: By appointment for group visits only Tue-Thur 1100 or 1400, when Mansion House functions permit; Closed Christmas, New Year, August and beginning of September
Admission: Free

⊖ Bank/Mansion House

This is the official residence of the Lord Mayor of London. Superb reception rooms and banqueting hall. Collection of porcelain, silver and gold dishes. Building dates to 18th century.

Monument
Monument Street, EC3
Tel: 01-626 2717

Open: 1 April-30 Sept, Mon-Fri 0900-1800, Sat & Sun 1400-1800; 1 Oct-31 March, Mon-Sat 0900-1400 & 1500-1600
Admission: Charge

⊖ Monument

This 202ft high, fluted Doric column designed by Wren to commemorate the Great Fire of London, stands 202ft from the outbreak of the fire in Pudding Lane. Panoramic view of London and the Thames can be enjoyed from the public balcony. There are 311 steps and no lifts.

Prince Henry's Room and Samuel Pepys Exhibition
17 Fleet Street, EC4
Tel: 01-353 7323

Open: 1345-1700 Mon-Fri, 1345-1630 Sat
Admission: Free

⊖ Temple

Dating from 1610, this is one of the few buildings in the City undamaged by the Great Fire. The original seventeenth century wood panelling and decorated ceiling are inscribed with the initials P H for Prince Henry who became Prince of Wales in 1610, the time the building was completed. On view is a collection of memorabilia of Samuel Pepys, the famous diarist, including an original letter to Charles II.

Roman Wall
Wakefield Gardens, Tower Hill, EC3

⊖ Tower Hill

Above street level, part of the mediaeval wall can be seen. The Roman Wall can only be seen from the sunken garden.

Royal Exchange
see London International Financial Futures Exchange.

Temple of Mithras
Queen Victoria Street, EC4

⊖ Mansion House

The remains of the temple dedicated to the Persian sun god adopted by the Romans have been reconstructed near the site where they were discovered.

The Temple
Two of the four Inns of Court are to be found in the City. They are the Inner Temple and Middle Temple. Founded in Mediaeval times, they still have the exclusive right to call persons to the Bar. It is possible to visit the ancient Hall of Middle Temple, (the Inner Temple Hall is open by appointment only) and Temple Church.

Inner Temple Hall, EC4
Open: By written application only: Sub Treasurer's Office, Honourable Society of Inner Temple, EC4 7HL

⊖ Temple

The Hall dates from 1955 and incorporates a Mediaeval Buttery and crypt.
A gateway leads to the Inner Temple from Fleet Street described as one of the best pieces of half timber work in London, above which is Prince Henry's Room, (see above).

Mansion House

continued overleaf

Temple Bar
Fleet Street, EC4
⊖ Aldwych/Temple

This marks the western boundary of the City. The original Temple Bar, designed by Sir Christopher Wren, was removed from its position in the middle of the road opposite the Law Courts in Victorian times to ease the traffic congestion it caused. It was replaced in 1880 by a monument which incorporates the figure of a bronze Griffin, the badge of the City. Wren's Temple Bar may return to the City one day from its temporary home at Theobald's Park, Herts.

Middle Temple Hall
Middle Temple Lane, EC4
Tel: 01-353 4355
Open: Mon-Fri 1000-1200 & 1500-1600. (Closed Aug, Christmas fortnight & week after Easter)
Admission: Free
⊖ Temple

Shakespeare is said to have taken part in a performance of "Twelfth Night" in this Elizabethan Hall, (mid-16th century), with its striking oak double hammerbeam roof, restored after the Second World War.

PLACES OF INTEREST

Lloyds of London (L)
Lime Street, EC3
Tel: 01-623 7100
Open: 1000-1600 Mon-Fri (excluding public holidays) (1400-1600 booked groups only). From 5th January '87 1000-1600 Mon-Fri (excluding public holidays) (1400-1600 booked groups only)
Admission: Free
⊖ Monument/Bank/Aldgate

International Insurance Market. The Visitors' Viewing Gallery, overlooks the famous Underwriting Room on four floors; the exhibition traces the history of Lloyds to the present day with a multimedia explanation of how Lloyds works. There is also a souvenir and coffee shop. The striking building designed by Richard Rodgers opened in 1986.

London International Financial Futures Exchange Ltd.
Royal Exchange, (between Threadneedle Street and Cornhill) EC3
Tel: 01-623 0444
Open: 1130-1345 Mon-Fri, (viewing area up to 20 persons only, groups must book in advance).
⊖ Bank

Open "outcry" market handling financial futures contracts and options contracts in history Royal Exchange – the third building on the site, (erected 1842-44). The first building was built by Sir Thomas Gresham (1564-70). The gilded grasshopper vane that graces the campanile of the current building is taken from Gresham's crest. The famous Leighton wall paintings can be seen on prior application only.

Stock Exchange (L)
Old Broad Street, EC2
Tel: 01-588 2355
Open: 0945-1515 Mon-Fri (Closed Bank Holidays)
⊖ Bank/Moorgate/Liverpool Street

Founded in 1801, the exchange moved to this site in 1970. It is the second largest exchange for stocks and shares in the world. Visitors can watch the proceedings from the visitor's gallery; those wishing to take advantage of the guided commentary and explanatory film should book in advance.

CHURCHES

All Hallows by the Tower
Byward Street, EC3
Tel: 01-481 2928
Open: Mon-Fri 0930-1800, Sat & Sun 1000-1800
Admission: Charge for Undercroft Musuem includes tour
♿ Access
⊖ Tower Hill

All Hallows was founded in the 7th century and survived the Great Fire. It was badly damaged in the Second World War; restoration work was completed in 1957. William Penn, founder of Pennsylvania was baptised here. In the Undercroft Museum there is a Roman pavement and Roman and Saxon artefacts. There is also a brass rubbing centre with 25 medieaval brasses; open Mon-Sat 1100-1745, Sun 1230-1745.

The Priory Church of St. Bartholomew the Great
57 West Smithfield, EC1
Tel: 01-606 1575
Open: Summer: Sun 0800-2030, Tue 1030-1730, other days 0830-1700; Winter: Sun 0800-2030, Tue 1030-1630, other days 0830-1600
Admission: Free
⊖ Barbican/St. Paul's

This Norman church was founded in 1123 by Rahere, a former courtier of Henry I and dedicated to St. Bartholomew who appeared to Rahere in a vision, curing him of illness. This is London's oldest church after the chapel at the White Tower. Regular concerts.

St. Brides
Fleet Street, EC4
Tel: 01-353 1301
Open: Mon-Sat 0830-1730, Sun 0830-2000
Admission: Free
& Access
⊖ Blackfriars

St. Bride's is the parish church of Fleet Street, and the newspaper world contributed generously to its restoration after extensive Second World War damage; archaeological excavation revealed its Roman origins. It was designed by Sir Christopher Wren and is dedicated to St. Bridget, from which its name is derived. The steeple has inspired the design of wedding cakes. Archaeological and printing exhibits in the crypt. Lunchtime recitals.

St. Giles Church
Cripplegate, Fore Street, Barbican, EC2
Tel: 01-606 3630
Open: Oct-March, daily (not Sat) 1000-1400; March-Oct, daily (not Sat) 1000-1700
Admission: Free but donations welcome

As with many of the City's churches, St. Giles has undergone its fair share of rebuilding and restoration work to the original 1390 building. Within the church grounds is a section of the Roman London Wall. Oliver Cromwell was married here and John Milton was buried here.

St. Paul's Cathedral
Ludgate Hill, EC4
Tel: 01-248 2705
Open: Mon-Sat 0900-1800. Crypt, Galleries & Ambulatory: Mon-Fri 1000-1615, Sat from 1100-1615, Sun – services only
Admission: Charge to Galleries, Crypt and Ambulatory. Church free, except to groups
& Access
⊖ St. Paul's/Mansion House

Wren's masterpiece St. Paul's stands on the site of Old St. Paul's destroyed in the Great Fire. A model of the former, huge church – 600ft long – can be seen in the crypt. Wren's new cathedral took from 1675 to 1710 to complete and is 515ft long and 365ft high (to the top of the cross). Wren is buried in the Crypt and on the tomb it says "If you seek his monument, look around". It is a remarkable building with important monuments to amongst others Admiral Lord Nelson and the Duke of Wellington who are buried here. The Whispering and Viewing Galleries give unrivalled views of London and of the paintings on the 200ft high dome (more than 600 steps). A cleaning and restoration programme is revealing the golden colour of the original Portland stone. This is the cathedral church of London with regular services (no sightseeing) and concerts. The wedding of the Prince and Princess of Wales took place here in 1981. Tours, bookshop.

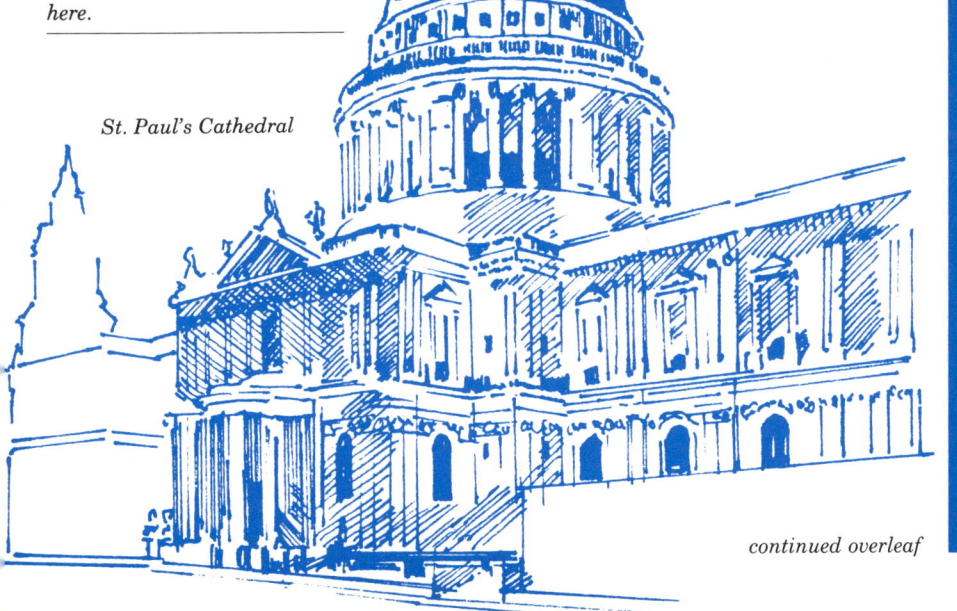

St. Paul's Cathedral

continued overleaf

Temple Church, EC4

Open: Daily 1000-1600 (except for Sunday services)

⊖ Temple/Blackfriars

This church serves the Middle and Inner Temples and is the most important of the five remaining round churches in England. It was first consecrated in 1185 and is exempt from episcopal jurisdiction. The church takes its name from the Crusading Order of the Knights Templar, founded in 1118 to protect pilgrims on their way to Jerusalem. Sir Christopher Wren married his first wife here in 1669.

ENTERTAINMENT

Barbican Centre (L)
Silk Street, Barbican, EC2
Box Office (1000-2000 Daily): 01-638 8891/ 628 8795. 24 hour Recorded Information: 01-628 2295/628 9760. Information: 01-638 4141

Open: Mon-Sat 0900-2300, Sun and Bank Holidays 1200-2300

♿ Access

⊖ Barbican (closed Sundays)/Moorgate

The Centre contains the Barbican Concert Hall (seats 2000), the Barbican Theatre (seats 1100) and smaller Pit Theatre, the Barbican Art Gallery (see separate entry), also a conservatory and restaurants, carvery style and self-service, there are also wine and coffee bars, and foyer bars.
This is the home of the Royal Shakespeare Company and the London Symphony Orchestra.

Mermaid Theatre (L)
Puddle Dock, EC4
Box Office Tel: 01-236 5568

⊖ Blackfriars

Theatre first established by Bernard Miles in 1956.

PARKS AND OPEN SPACES

The City is responsible for several parks and open spaces outside its own area, including Epping Forest and Highgate Wood. Within the City however, the largest garden is Finsbury Circus. Others are Postman's Park, a former churchyard of St. Botolph Church, so called as it was used by employees of the former main post office opposite; St. Dunstan's in the East – cultivated gardens in a former churchyard; Tower Hill Terrace by the Tower of London; Cleary Gardens by Queen Victoria Street and St. Swithin's (Salters Hall Court). These gardens are open from 0800 until half an hour before dusk. (Latest closing time; 2130).

MARKETS

Leadenhall Market
Leadenhall Street, EC3
Open: Mon-Fri 0700-1600. Best times: Early; lunchtime

⊖ Bank/Monument

Game; poultry; fish; meat.

Smithfield Market
Smithfield, EC1
Tel: 01-236 8734
Open: Mon-Fri 0500-1200

⊖ Farringdon/Barbican
Night bus: N83, N89

London's principal wholesale meat, poultry, and game market in historic Smithfield once used for fairs and tournaments; also place of execution in the 16th century.

Spitalfields Market
Spitalfields, E1
Tel: 01-247 7331
Open: Mon-Fri 0430-1100, Sat 0430-0900 (approx.)

⊖ Liverpool Street
Night bus: N84

Wholesale fruit; vegetable and flower market in an area where many silk weavers lived (see p. 51).

ISLINGTON

The London Borough of Islington borders the City and the boroughs of Hackney, Haringey and Camden. It includes the two former Metropolitan Boroughs of Finsbury and Islington and is covered in detail in LVCB's *Exploring Outer London* guide (see page 64). In this volume, Clerkenwell, rich in history and traditions is explored.

Clerkenwell takes its name from the Clerks' Well discovered in 1924 in what is now the New Statesman building. It was called the Clerks' Well after the parish clerks of the City of London, who, in the Middle Ages, performed their "Miracle Plays" near this site on the banks of the river Fleet. The well is more than one thousand years old and can be visited on application.

Clerkenwell originally grew up around the 12th century Benedictine Nunnery of St. Mary's and the Priory of the Order of St. John of Jerusalem. St. Mary's was destroyed as a result of the Dissolution of the Monasteries ordered by Henry VIII. The Gatehouse and the Norman Crypt remain of the Priory, which was named after the English Order of the Knights of St. John. They cared for pilgrims and the sick. The Museum of the Order of St. John which traces the history of the pioneers of First Aid training, the St. John Ambulance Association and the Ambulance Brigade now occupies the Gate House.

Between 1347 and 1350, England's population may well have halved as people fell victim to the fearful "Black Death," or Bubonic Plague. In overcrowded London, the spread of the disease was rapid. In Clerkenwell, Sir Walter de Manny founded the Charterhouse as a centre of prayer for the victims. Carthusian monks lived here as did Sir Thomas More as a young man. Later it became a palace visited by Queen Elizabeth I and at the beginning of the 17th century, a boys' school was founded here. In 1872 the school moved out to Surrey. Sadly, most of the old buildings were destroyed during the Second World War; the surviving parts are occupied by the Charterhouse Pensioners, and can be visited.

The fertile meadowland on which Clerkenwell was founded and the purity of the water in its wells attracted amongst others, Gordon's Gin distillery which still stands on the site of the well of 1769. The headquarters of Samuel Whitbread's Brewery in Chiswell Street occupies the same buildings in which it was founded in the 18th century.

There is still a well under the Sadlers Wells Theatre in Rosebery Avenue, which was founded in 1683. The present building dates from 1927 and was founded by Lillian Baylis, owner of the Old Vic Theatre.

continued overleaf

ISLINGTON

Clerkenwell Green was once the centre of a semi-rural village and in the 17th century was surrounded by the smart houses of the nobility. The Marx Memorial Library, in commemorating the 50th anniversary of Karl Marx's death, was founded in 1933 in the oldest building on Clerkenwell Green originally built as a charity school in 1737, later becoming a radical working men's club. Lenin wrote here from 1902 to 1903.

Clerkenwell has a large Italian community in the area known as "Little Italy". St. Peter's, built in 1863, was the first Italian church to be built outside Italy.

A major annual event in "Little Italy" is the procession which takes place around the streets of Clerkenwell in July, on the Sunday after the "Feast of Our Lady of Mount Carmel" then followed by a traditional fete or "Sagra". The Clerkenwell Festival is also held in July.

After a period of decline, business and workshops are returning to the area. There are some five hundred crafts and other workshops, many of which can be visited by special arrangement.

Tours of Clerkenwell operate every day at 1430 hours with an additional tour on Sundays at 1100 hours.

For further information contact: Clerkenwell Heritage Centre (Islington Visitor Bureau), 33-35 St. John's Square, EC1M 4DN. Tel: 01-250 1039. Open: April-Sept Mon-Fri 0900-1800, Sat & Sun 1400-1700, Oct-March Mon-Fri 1000-1700.

St. John's Gate

PLACES OF INTEREST

HISTORIC BUILDINGS/HOUSES

Charterhouse
Tel: 01-253 9503
Open: Wed 1445 (April-July) for guided tours
Admission: Charge
⊖ Barbican (closed Sundays)

Carthusian monks founded Charterhouse which derived its name from Chartreuse in France where the order was founded. Charterhouse public school now in Godalming, Surrey was originally here. The original building dates mainly from the 16th century.

Clerks Well
14-16 Farringdon Lane, EC1
Tel: 01-609 3051 Ext. 65 (Farringdon Public Library)
Open: By advance booking only. Contact: Finsbury Public Library. Mon, Tues & Thurs 0900-2000; Wed & Fri 0900-1300; Sat 0900-1700 Tel: no. as above)

Mediaeval well from which Clerkenwell takes its name. Discovered in 1924, the Well has been restored and now has a viewing gallery.

Marx Memorial Library
Marx House, 37A Clerkenwell Green, EC1
Tel: 01-253 1485
Open: Mon & Fri 1400-1800, Tue, Wed & Thu 1400-2100, Sat 1100-1300
Admission: Free
⊖ Farringdon

The Library, housed in the oldest building on Clerkenwell Green, contains 100,000 books, pamphlets and periodicals. It was formerly a Socialist Press, the first in Britain, and Lenin printed his journal "Iskra" here.

Society of Genealogists
14 Charterhouse Buildings, Goswell Road, EC1
Tel: 01-251 8799
Open: 1000-1800 Tues, Fri, Sat 1000-2000 Wed & Thurs
Admission: Charge
⊖ Barbican

The Society's library contains records from 1538 to 1837 including parish register copies and monumental inscriptions – Open to research into family history.

The Tower of the Charterhouse

Wesley's House and the Museum of Methodism
47 City Road, EC1
Tel: 01-253 2262
Open: Mon-Sat 1000-1600; Sun after 1100 service & lunch followed by brief talk by the Historian
Admission: Charge
⊖ Old Street

Original 18th century house in which John Wesley lived and died. Illustrates the beginnings of methodism. Beneath the Chapel is Museum of Methodism (see separate entry).

Museum of Methodism
49 City Road, EC1
Tel: 01-253 2262
Open: Mon-Sat 1000-1600, Sun – after 1100 service & lunch followed by brief talk by the historian
Admission: Charge
⊖ Old Street

The museum is housed in the crypt of Wesley's chapel. Illustrates the development of Methodism from 18th century to the present day.

continued overleaf

ISLINGTON

Beer delivery using a traditional dray

Whitbread Stables (L)
The Brewery, Garrett Street, EC1
Tel: 01-606 4455 Ext. 2534
Open: By appointment only 1100-1230 and 13300-1500 Mon-Fri
Admission: Charge
♿ Access
⊖ Barbican (closed Sunday)/Moorgate

The Whitbread Brewery Shire Horses are still used on the morning round to deliver beer to pubs in the City. They also appear on ceremonial occasions such as the Lord Mayor's Show. A Farrier is at work and there is a gift shop (open 0900-1700 Mon-Fri)

Library and Museum of the Order of St. John
St. John's Gate, St. John's Lane, EC1
Tel: 01-253 6644 Ext. 35
Open: Tue & Fri 1000-1800, Sat 1000-1600; Closed Bank Holiday Weekends & Christmas Week
Admission: Free but donations welcome
⊖ Farringdon

This 16th century Gatehouse and 12th century crypt contains paintings, silver, a library and insignia and treasures of the Knights of St. John.

CHURCHES

St. Peter's Italian Church
Clerkenwell Road, EC1
⊖ Farringdon

The first Italian Church to be build outside Italy, St. Peter's was built in 1863. It is the focal point of the large Italian community's annual fete or "Sagra" which marks the feast of Our Lady of Mount Carmel.

St. James
Clerkenwell Close, EC1
⊖ Farringdon

Parish Church of Clerkenwell, built by James Carr in 1792 on the site of the 12th century Nunnery of St. Mary, the remains of which can be seen in the gardens behind the church. The church contains one of the finest organs in London.

ENTERTAINMENT

Sadler's Wells Theatre
Rosebery Avenue, EC1
Tel: 01-278 8916 (Box Office)

Formerly the home of the English National Opera Company (now based at the London Coliseum) the theatre still stages opera and ballet performed by visiting companies.

PARKS AND OPEN SPACES

Bunhill Fields Burial Ground
City Road, EC1
⊖ Old Street

A Pre-historic burial ground known as "Bone Hill" from which its name is derived; it was used to bury victims of the plague of 1665. It has been closed as a burial ground since the middle of the 19th century.

SPORTS CENTRES

Finsbury Leisure Centre
Norman Street, EC1
Tel: 01-253 2346/4490
⊖ Old Street

Sports Hall, weight training, outdoor tennis courts.

TOWER HAMLETS

⊖ Tower Hill (Circle and District lines)

The London Borough of Tower Hamlets takes its name from the Tower of London, located within its boundaries. In the 16th century, men from the settlements, or "Hamlets", nearest to the Tower were mustered to perform guard duty there. The Borough today contains the three former metropolitan boroughs of Bethnal Green, Poplar and Stepney. LVCB's guide *Exploring Outer London* has more detail (see page 64).

The Roman presence is still evident in the borough. The Roman Road follows the ancient route into London from the important Roman settlement at Colchester. The Romans also built a fortified wall around the City – the London Wall. Sections of it can still be seen today, on Tower Hill and by the Wardrobe Tower and Wakefield Gardens at the Tower of London. It is possible to "Walk the London Wall" using the Museum of London's specially prepared map (see page 41).

In the late 17th and early 18th centuries, Tower Hamlets saw a large influx of French Huguenots, who fled the oppressive regimes of their own country bringing with them new skills. They were renowned silkweavers and settled predominently in the Spitalfields area, named after the Augustinian Hospital or "spital" of St. Mary. Several of their houses can still be seen today in Fournier Street. Three churches, of which the borough is justly proud, were built by Nicholas Hawksmoor, including Christ Church in Commercial Street. In the early part of this century the clothing trade was dominant in Whitechapel and Spitalfields following the arrival of Jewish immigrants who, like the Huguenots, were fleeing religious persecution.

London's trade was carried out in quays along the Pool of London and the first enclosed dock was completed in 1802 in the Isle of Dogs, followed by many others so that by the mid-19th century, the Isle of Dogs was Europe's largest shipbuilding centre. It was here that the great engineer Isambard Kingdom Brunel worked on the steamship "The Great Eastern". The docks continued as thriving centres for boat building and cargo handling well into this century. The advent of container delivery after the Second World War favoured Tilbury and other ports and London's docklands declined. Redevelopment started in the '60's with St. Katharine Dock, which has become an attractive yacht haven with the Dickens Inn, the World Trade Centre and Tower Hotel. Further developments are under way on the Isle of Dogs; The Docklands Light Railway, due to open in July

continued overleaf

TOWER HAMLETS

1987 will provide a spectacular ride from Tower Hill (The Minories) above the West India Dock to Island Gardens opposite Greenwich. For information contact the London Docklands Development Corporation (Tel: 01-513 3000).

London as the nation's leading port will be documented in a new Museum in Docklands, scheduled to open in 1988. A preview of the museum's wealth of exhibits, in W Warehouse in the Royal Victoria Dock, can be arranged by contacting the Museum in Docklands team at the Museum of London Tel: 01-600 3699.

Tobacco Dock in Wapping, formerly a tobacco warehouse, is currently being developed as a "Shopping Village" to serve the east of London. The first phase of building is due for completion in 1987.

Opposite St. Katharine's, near the Tower of London, the site of the Royal Mint is being redeveloped. A museum to house the remains of the 14th century Cistercian Abbey of St. Mary Graces which stood on this site may be included in the plans for offices and shops.

For further information contact: Tower Hamlets Tourist Information Centre, 88 Roman Road, E2. Tel: 01-980 3749, 01-980 4831 ext. 211. Mon-Fri 0900-1730.

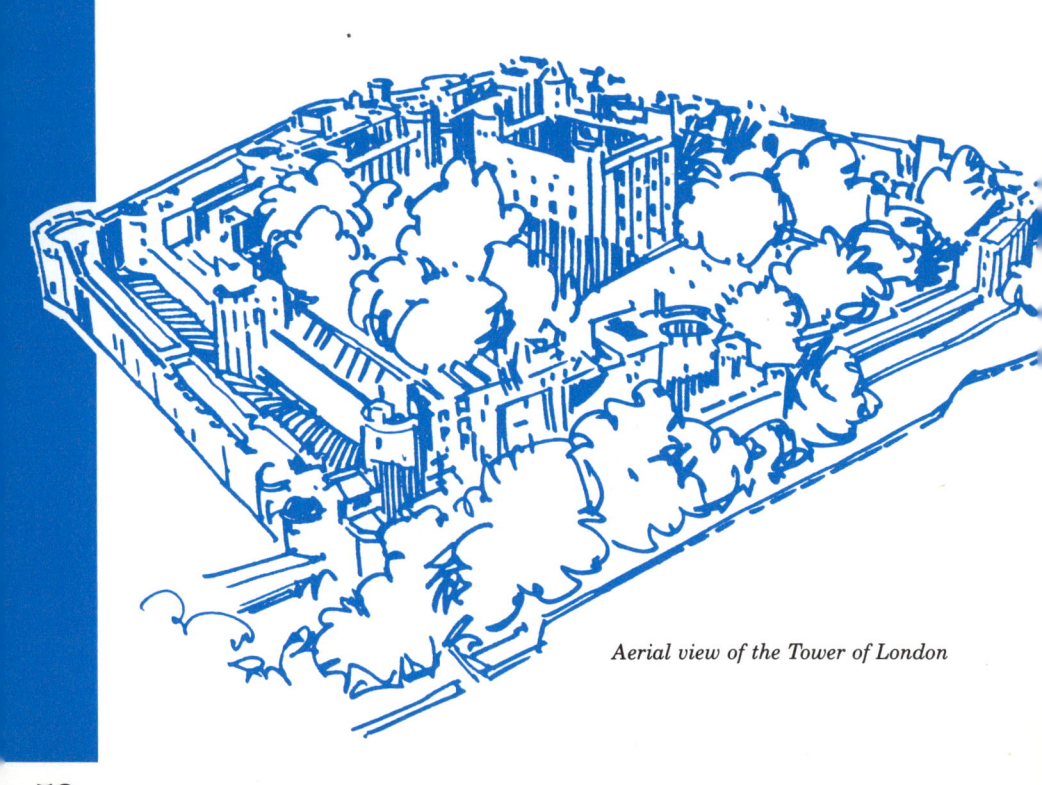

Aerial view of the Tower of London

PLACES OF INTEREST

TOWER HAMLETS

ART GALLERIES

Whitechapel Art Gallery
80 Whitechapel High Street, E1
Tel: 01-377 0107
Open: Tue-Sun 1100-1700, Wed 1100-2000
Admission: Charge for Lecture Theatre
↔ Aldgate East

Housed behind a striking Art Nouveau front, the gallery offers a wide range of temporary exhibition of modern art. Lecture theatre; Cafeteria.

MUSEUMS

Bethnal Green Museum of Childhood
Cambridge Heath Road, E2
Tel: 01-980 2415
Open: Mon-Thur & Sat 1000-1800, Sun 1430-1800 (Closed Fri, 24-26 Dec, 1 Jan, May Day)
Admission: Free
♿ Access by prior arrangement
↔ Bethnal Green

Toys, dolls, dolls houses and games through the ages. Children's costumes. Puppets and toy theatres. (Run by the Victoria & Albert Museum).

Dennis Severs' House
18 Folgate Street, EC2
Tel: 01-247 4013
↔ Liverpool Street

Mr. Severs gives tours of this 18th century former silk-weavers' house decorated with period furniture and decor. (Three hours).

Herald Museum
see Tower of London

National Museum of Labour History
The Old Limehouse Town Hall, Commercial Road, E14
Tel: 01-515 3229
Open: Tue-Sat 0930-1700, Sun 1430-1730
Admission: Free
↔ Aldgate East then Bus 5 or 15

The history of the growth and development of the trade unions and socialism, told through pictorial and documentary exhibits. The museum contains a banner collection and photographs dating from 1840's of social and labour history. Reference library. Lectures.

Royal Fusiliers Museum
see Tower of London

CHURCHES

Chapel Royal of St. Peter Ad Vincula
Tower Bridge, Tower Hill, EC3
Tel: 01-709 0765
Open: Sun 0915 Holy Communion, 1100 Matins and Sermon; closed August
Admission: Free
↔ Tower Hill

Built in the reign of King Henry I for the use of the Tower's garrison, servants and prisoners.

Christchurch
Commercial Street, Spitalfields, E1
Tel: 01-247 7202
↔ Aldgate East, Liverpool Street

Built in 1729 by Nicholas Hawksmoor (first pupil and then partner of Sir Christopher Wren). It has an unusual octagonal tower. Spitalfields Music Festival takes place here in June.

PARKS AND OPEN SPACES

King Edward Memorial Park
The Highway, E1
Open: 0930-dusk (approx)
↔ Shadwell

Covering 8,500 acres, this riverside park marks the site of the old Shadwell fish market. There are gardens, recreation facilities, including a children's playground and refreshments.

SPORTS CENTRES

Sedgwick Sports Centre (L)
10 Whitechapel High Street, E1
Tel: 01-481 5123
↔ Aldgate East

Multi-sports hall, squash courts and multi-gym.

Spitalfields (Brady) Centre
192-196 Hanbury Street, E1
Tel: 01-247 0346
↔ Whitechapel

Two indoor sports halls, weight-training.

Wapping Centre
Tench Street, E1
Tel: 01-488 9421/22
↔ Wapping

Indoor sports hall.

continued overleaf

TOWER HAMLETS

MARKETS

The East End has several good markets. Many are open on Sundays, as this is where Jewish families settled when they first came to London and they were given permission to trade on the Christian "day of rest". The markets retain their cockney flavours – with the added influence of Bangladeshi's who have settled in this area since the 1950's.

Brick Lane, E1, E2
Open: Sun 0700-1400
⊖ Liverpool Street/Aldgate East
Second hand goods; clothes.

Columbia Road
Shoreditch, E2
Open: Sun 0700-1400
⊖ Liverpool Street
Plants; garden fittings; equipment etc.

Petticoat Lane, E1
Open: Sun 0900-1400 (also open weekdays in Wentworth Street for fruit & veg 1030-1430)
Best times: Early Sunday
⊖ Liverpool Street
Clothes; household goods.

Petticoat Lane Designer Fashion Market (L)
(Between Middlesex St. and Goulston Street), EC1
Open: Sun 0700-1400
⊖ Aldgate East/Liverpool Street
Covered fashion market part of main market.

Roman Road
Bow, E3
Open: Tue & Thur 1000-1400 and all day Sat 1000-1700
Best time: Sat
⊖ Bethnal Green
Clothes; shoes; food; fancy goods.

Whitechapel (Waste)
Whitechapel Road, E1
Open: Mon-Sat 0830-1730 (half day Thur)
⊖ Whitechapel
Fruit; flowers; Waste (Sat only) house hold goods and clothes.

Billingsgate Market
87 West India Dock Road, E14
Open: Tue-Sat 0530-0900
⊖ Mile End, then buses D1 & 277
London's principal wholesale fish market which moved here from Upper Thames Street in 1982.

HISTORIC BUILDINGS/HOUSES

Tower of London
Tower Hill, EC3
Tel: 01-709 0765
Open: Mar-Oct, Mon-Sat 0930-1745, last admission 1700, Sun 1400-1745, last admission 1700; Nov-Feb, Mon-Sat 0930-1630, last admission 1600, Sun closed all day. Crown jewels closed Feb.
Admission: Charge
⊖ Tower Hill

The Tower of London is a fortress surrounded by a moat now filled in as a public garden, and has two walls. The Inner Wall walk links the separate towers and can be reached from Wakefield Tower. The White Tower was built for William the Conqueror and served as palace, fortress, state prison and the place of execution. The Tower also housed the Royal Armouries and Crown Jewels – still on display, and at one time included the Royal Mint, Royal Observatory, Public Records and the first Zoo. Only the black ravens remain – the legend is that England and the Tower are doomed to collapse should they leave.
St. John's Chapel in the White Tower is the oldest church in London. The collection of arms and armour in the White Tower is unrivalled. The Crown Jewels include regalia dating from the Restoration.
The Tower also includes two separate museums:
The Royal Fusiliers Museum illustrating the history of this regiment with uniforms, medals and equipment.
The Heralds' Museum shows dress uniforms and tabards, shields and crests.
The Yeoman Warders, in their historic costume dating to the time of Henry VII, are known as Beefeaters and give frequent tours during opening hours. They also perform ceremonial duties. The Changing of the Guard ceremony takes place every day at the Tower at 1200 by the same regiment as at Buckingham Palace. The Ceremony of the Keys takes place each evening to keep the Tower safe from attack. The public may watch this, apply in writing well in advance to the Resident Governor, Queen's House, HM Tower of London, EC3N 4AB. (See also Traditional London p. 64).

OTHER PLACES OF INTEREST

St. Katharine's Dock, E1
🚇 Tower Hill

The first of London's docks to be transformed into a commercial, housing and leisure centre. Yachts are moored in St. Katharine's Marina; the Dickens Inn in an old warehouse has a bar and two restaurants. Ivory House is the only remaining original warehouse designed by Hardwick, with apartments, shops and a cabaret restaurant, the Beefeater; the World Trade Centre offers facilities for new companies in London; the Tower Hotel, overlooks the Thames; the new London Commodity Exchange is housed in a replica of the old warehouse on this spot.

The Historic Ships Collection is closed. Only two of the ships will remain, they are the "Nore" and the "Challenge". The Kathleen and May is open to the public on the south bank (see p. 58). RRS Discovery is now in Dundee.

Tower Bridge, SE1 **(L)**
Tel: 01-403 3761
Open: 1 April-31 Oct, 1000-1830, last entry 1745; 1 Nov-31 Mar, 1000-1645, last entry 1600
Admission: Charge
🚇 Tower Hill

This major landmark opened in 1894, was designed to match the nearby Tower of London. The walkways opened to the public in 1982. In the north-west tower an exhibition illustrates the building of the bridge. The south tower shows a display of the City's bridges and a model of Tower Bridge. From the walkway 60ft up there are excellent views of London. To the south of the bridge is a museum with the original steam engines used to lift the bridge.

TOWER HAMLETS

Tower Bridge

SOUTHWARK

The London Borough of Southwark stretches from the river Thames in the north to Dulwich in the south. The areas of Bermondsey, Camberwell, Dulwich, Herne Hill, Peckham, Rotherhithe and Walworth are covered in detail in LCVB's *Exploring Outer London* guide (see page 64).

Northern Southwark's strategic position on the River Thames made it an important settlement since Roman times. The first bridge across the Thames was built here in the First Century AD. From the 9th century onwards Southwark was a religious centre with many churches and monasteries including the cathedral church of St. Saviour and St. Mary Overie founded by the Augustinians. It has been frequently rebuilt and in 1905 it became Southwark Cathedral.

The Bishops of Winchester were based in Southwark, which was free of the constraints of the City of London across the river. So the theatre flourished and the Bankside area became well known for its sometimes dubious entertainment. Shakespeare's "Globe" theatre once stood here and will be recreated by the film producer Sam Wanamaker in the next few years.

Until 1750, London Bridge was the only bridge across the Thames, making Southwark the main entry point into London from the south. Along Borough High Street which leads to the bridge, there were many Inns to cater for the travellers' needs. Today, the "George Inn", the only galleried pub in London, is the sole survivor. During the Summer, performances of Shakespeare's plays are given outside in the Inn's yard. Most of the Inns went out of business with the advent of the railways which replaced coaches and horses. London Bridge station was the first to be built in London in 1836.

In the 18th and 19th centuries, wharves and docks lined the riverbank of Southwark, and the commercial centre prospered. Foodstuffs were stored in the riverside wharves around Tooley Street, between London Bridge and Tower Bridge – it became known as "London's Larder". With the closure of the docks after the Second World War these areas fell into rapid decline.

Hays Wharf in Bermondsey between London Bridge and Tower Bridge was the oldest in the Port of London and is currently undergoing redevelopment as part of the London Bridge City Scheme. It is Europe's largest commercial riverside development and, as well as providing office space, the area will also include a landscaped riverside walk, a new pier for ferry services and a shopping arcade, to be called Hay's Galleria (due to open in 1987). St. Mary Overie Dock has been filled in and redeveloped in the style of the old buildings; it houses the Schooner Kathleen and May.

The Boilerhouse Project, formerly at the Victoria & Albert Museum, which illustrates the history, theory and practice of industrial design, will open as a Museum of Design in 1988 in new premises at Butlers Wharf, SE1 opposite St. Katharine's Dock.

Reputedly the oldest fruit and vegetable market in London is Borough Market. In the 17th century, its sprawling mass extended from London Bridge to St. Margaret's Hill causing such traffic congestion that it was decided that the market should have a permanent site. Further south, antique collectors and dealers head for the New Caledonian or Bermondsey Markets in Tower Bridge Road each, Friday morning.

For further information contact: Public Relations Department (Information Section), Town Hall, Peckham Road SE5 8UB. Tel: 01-703 6311. Open: Mon-Thurs 0900-1700, (Fri 0900-1645).

PLACES OF INTEREST

ART GALLERIES

Bankside Gallery
48 Hopton Street, Blackfriars, SE1
Tel: 01-928 7521
Open: During exhibitions, Tue-Sat 1000-1700, Sun 1400-1800
Admission: Charge
♿ Access
⊖ Blackfriars

The Gallery is the home of the Royal Society of Painters in Watercolours and The Royal Society of Painter-Etchers and Engravers and holds regular changing exhibitions of watercolours and prints.

MUSEUMS

Shakespeare Globe Museum
1 Bear Gardens, Bankside, SE1
Tel: 01-928 6342
Open: Tues-Sat 1000-1730, Sun 1400-1800. (Please ring bell to gain admission)
Admission: Charge
⊖ London Bridge

Elizabethan theatre history from 1550-1642 with models and replicas of the Globe and Cockpit playhouses. A plaque on the wall marks the approximate site of the famous Globe Theatre where Shakespeare himself is said to have acted. The new Globe theatre is being built nearby.

London Dungeon
28/34 Tooley Street, SE1
Tel: 01-403 0606
Open: 1 April-30 Sep, Daily 1000-1730; 1 Oct-31 Mar, Daily 1000-1630
Admission: Charge
♿ Access
⊖ London Bridge

Exhibition of British Medieaval History depicting torture, death, damnation and disease. Life-size tableaux with eerie sound effects and lighting. Not suitable for children under 10 years.

Operating Theatre
(Old St. Thomas'), The Chapter House, St. Thomas Street, SE1
Tel: 01-407 7600 Ext. 2739
Open: Feb 1987-Dec 1987 Mon, Wed & Fri 1230-1600, Tue & Thu after 1130 by appointment only for groups
Admission: Charge
⊖ London Bridge

Restored 1822 women's operating theatre is the only 19th century operating theatre in England. Exhibits tell the story of surgery, herbal medicine.

continued overleaf

TOWER HAMLETS

HISTORIC BUILDINGS

The George Inn
Borough High Street, SE1
Tel: 01-407 2056

⊖ London Bridge

The only remaining galleried inn in London. Dickens mentioned it in "Little Dorrit" and Shakespeare is said to have acted here. In the Summer, his plays are performed in the courtyard. The inn also has a restaurant and a rare "Inn-Keeper's" clock dating from 1676.

CHURCHES

Southwark Cathedral
London Bridge, SE1
Tel: 01-407 2939
Admission: Free

⊖ London Bridge

The Cathedral and Collegiate church of St. Saviour and St. Mary Overie, is the oldest Gothic church in London dating from 606. The present building was built in the 15th century and partly rebuilt in 1890. Points of interest include the Harvard Chapel, a magnificent altar screen and retro choir and interesting memorials including the Shakespeare memorial window (his brother was buried here).

SPORTS CENTRES

Colombo Street Sports and Community Centre
Colombo Street, Blackfriars, SE1
Tel: 01-261 1658

⊖ Blackfriars

Indoor sports hall, weight-training, indoor bowls and roller-skating.

MARKETS

Bermondsey Antique Market (L)
(corner of Long Lane and Bermondsey Street), SE1
Open: Friday 0500-1400

⊖ London Bridge

Covered market. Glass; silver; brass; maps and prints.

Borough Market
Cathedral Street, SE1
Tel: 01-407 1002
Open: Mon-Sat 0200-1000

⇌ London Bridge
Night Bus: N89

Oldest municipal fruit, vegetable and flower market in Britain.

New Caledonian Market
Tower Bridge Road, SE1
Open: Fri 0700-1400
Best times: Before 12 noon

⊖/⇌ London Bridge

Main market for dealers in all types of antiques. Including Bermondsey Antique Market.

HISTORIC SHIPS

HMS Belfast
Symon's Wharf, Vine Lane, Tooley Street, SE1
Tel: 01-407 6434

Open: 20 Mar-31 Oct Daily 1100-1750, 1 Nov-19 Mar Daily 1100-1630; Closed New Year's Day, Good Friday, First Monday in May, 24, 25, 26 Dec
Admission: Charge

⊖ London Bridge/Tower Hill

This 11,350 tonnes World War II Cruiser is now a museum containing an exhibition on Battleships and D-Day. The main features are the gun turrets and navigation bridge. A ferry service operates between Tower Pier and H.M.S. Belfast.

Kathleen and May Schooner
Cathedral Street, SE1
Tel: 01-403 3965

Open: 31 Mar-31 Oct Daily 1000-1600; 1 Nov-30 Mar 1100-1500. (Closed 24-26 Dec & New Years Eve and New Year's Day)
Admission: Charge

⊖ London Bridge

Wooden Top Sail Schooner afloat in an enclosed dock. Exhibition onboard.

HMS Belfast

SUBJECT INDEX

Antiques
Antiquarius	13
Bermondsey Antique Market	58
Bond Street Antique Centre	24
Chenil Galleries	13
Earls Court Exhibition Centre Sunday Market	13
Gray's Antique Market	24
Gray's Mews Antique Market	24
Jubilee Market	31
London Silver Vaults	37
New Caledonian Market	58
Petticoat Lane Market	54
Portobello Road Market (Sat)	13

Armour
Wallace Collection	18
White Tower (Tower of London)	54

Art
Barbican Art Gallery	40
Bankside Gallery	57
Courtauld Institute Galleries	33
Hayward Gallery	30
Institute of Contemporary Art	17
Leighton House	11
Mall Galleries	17
National Gallery	17
National Portrait Gallery	18
Percival David Foundation	34
Queen's Gallery	18
Royal Academy	18
Saatchi Collection	18
Serpentine Gallery	18
Tate Gallery	18
Thomas Coram Foundation	34
Wallace Collection	18
Whitechapel Art Gallery	53
Zamana Gallery	9

Aviation
Science Museum	10

Famous People's Houses
Apsley House	20
Baden Powell House	9
Carlyle's House	10
Dicken's House	35
Dr. Johnson's House	41
Linley Sambourne House	11
Sir John Soane's Museum	35
Wesley's House	49

Fashion
Court Dress Collection (Kensington Palace)	11
Jubilee Market	24
Kensington Market	13
Petticoat Lane Designer Fashion Market	54
Victoria and Albert Museum	10

London History
Guildhall	42
London Dungeon	57
London Experience	21
Museum of London	41
Shakespeare Globe Museum	57
Tower of London	54

Maritime History
H.M.S. Belfast	58
Kathleen and May Schooner	58
Science Museum	10

Medicine
Chelsea Physic Garden	12
Faraday's Laboratory	19
Operating Theatre – Old St. Thomas'	57
Science Museum (Wellcome Museum of the History of Medicine)	10

Military
Heralds Museum (Tower of London)	54
National Army Museum	9
Royal Fusiliers Museum (Tower of London)	54

Musical Instruments
Museum of Instruments	9

Philately
National Postal Museum	41

Sports Centres
Chelsea Sports Centre	12
Colombo St. Sports and Community Centre	58
Finsbury Leisure Centre	50
Fitness Centre	25
Jubilee Hall Recreation Centre	25
Kensington New Pools	12
Marshall Street Centre	25
Oasis Sports Centre	37
Paddington Recreation Ground	25
Porchester Centre	25
Queen Mother's Sports Centre	25
Sanctuary (Ladies only)	25
Sedgwick Sports Centre	53
Spitalfields (Brady) Centre	53
Wapping Centre	53
Westbourne Green Sports Complex	25

Theatres
Full Theatre List	26
Shakespeare Globe Museum	57
Theatre Museum	20
Theatre Tours – Contact LVCB for details	

Transport and Technology
London Toy and Model Museum	19
London Transport Museum	19
Royal Mews	22
Science Museum	10
Telecom Technology Showcase	41

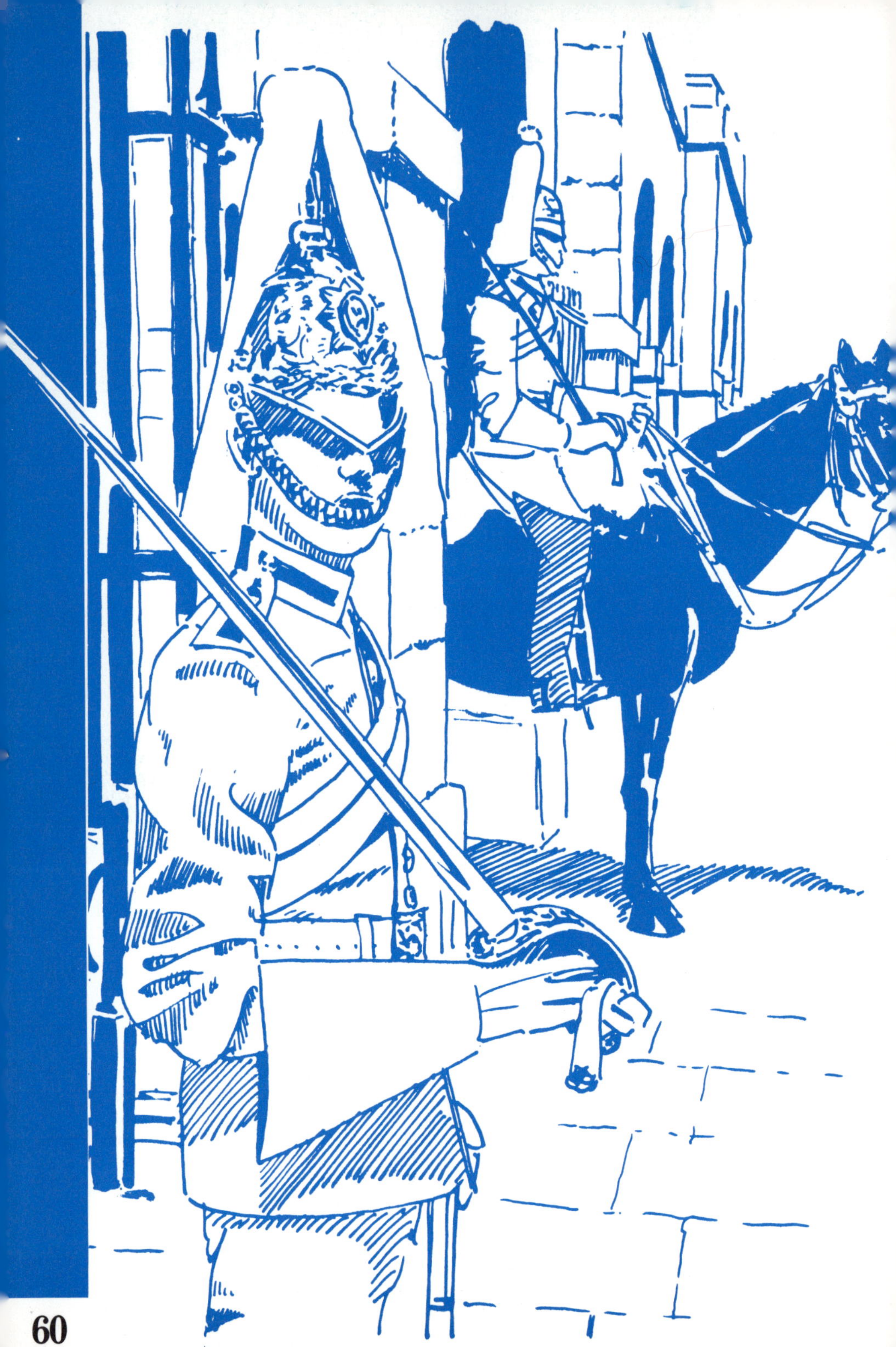

INDEX

All Hallows by the Tower	44
Antiquarius	13
Apsley House	20
Archbishops Park	31
Baden Powell House	9
Bank of England	38
Bankside Gallery	57
Banqueting House	14, 20
Barbican Art Gallery	40
Barbican Centre	40, 46
Barbican Theatre	26
Beating Retreat	16
H.M.S. Belfast	58
Bermondsey Antique Market	58
Berwick Street Market	24
Bethnal Green Museum of Childhood	53
Billingsgate Market	54
Bloomsbury Theatre	33
Boilerhouse Project (See Museum of Design)	57
Bond Street Antique Centre	24
Borough Market	57, 58
Brick Lane Market	54
British Crafts Centre	17
British Library	34
British Museum	34
British Telecom Tower	33
Brompton Oratory	11
Bunhill Fields	50
Cabinet War Rooms	19
Camden Arts Festival	33
Canal Trips (See River and Canal Trips)	5
Capital Card	4
Carlyle's House	10
Central Criminal Court (Old Bailey)	38, 41
Chapel Royal of St. Peter Ad Vincula	53
Charterhouse	47, 49
Changing the Guard	16
Chelsea Old Church	7, 12
Chelsea Physic Garden	8, 12
Chelsea Sports Centre	12
Chenil Galleries	13
"China Town"	15
Christchurch	51, 53
Church Street Market	24
City of London Festival	40
Clerkenwell Festival	48
Clerks Well	47, 49
Colombo Street Sports and Community Centre	58
Columbia Road Market	54
Commonwealth Institute	9
Coram Fields	37
Courtauld Institute Galleries	33
Court Dress Collection (See Kensington Palace)	11
Crafts Council Gallery	17
Cricket Memorial Gallery	15, 19
Crosby Hall	10
Dennis Severs House	53
Design Centre	17
Dickens House	35
Docklands	51
Drill Hall	33
Drapers Hall	42
Earls Court Exhibition Centre Sunday Market	13
Faraday's Laboratory and Museum	19
Festival of Street Theatre	14
Finsbury Leisure Centre	50
Fishmongers Hall	42
Fitness Centre	25
George Inn	56, 58
Geological Museum	9
Goldsmiths Hall	42
Grays Antique Market	24
Grays Mews Antique Market	24
Grays Inn	36
Grays Inn Fields	37
Green Park	24
Guards Chapel	22
Guildhall	40, 42
Guildhall Clock Museum	40
Guinness World of Records	21
Haberdashers' Hall	42
Half Price Ticket Booth	28
Hays Galleria	56
Hayward Gallery	30
Herald Museum (See Tower of London)	54
Holland Park	12
House of St. Barnabas in Soho	20
Houses of Parliament	20
Hyde Park	24
Inner Temple Hall	43
Institute of Contemporary Arts	17
Jewel Tower	20
Jewish Museum	35
Dr. Johnson's House	41
Jubilee Gardens	31
Jubilee Hall	25
Jubilee Market	24
Kathleen and May Schooner	58

INDEX

Kensington Gardens	12
Kensington Market	13
Kensington New Pools	12
Kensington Palace	7, 11
King Edward Memorial Park	53
Laserium	21
Leadenhall Market	46
Leather Lane Market	37
Leighton House Museum and Art Gallery	11
Library and Museum of the Order of St. John	47, 50
Light Fantastic Gallery of Holography	17
Light Fantastic – World Centre of Holography	17
Lincoln's Inn	36
Lincoln's Inn Fields	37
Linley Sambourne House	11
"Little Italy"	48
Livery Halls	39, 42
Lloyds of London	38, 44
London Bridge City Scheme	56
London Contemporary Dance (See Place Theatre)	33
London Diamond Centre	21
London Docklands Development Corporation	52
London Docklands Light Railway	39, 51
London Dungeon	57
London Experience	21
London Explorer Pass	4
London International Financial Futures Exchange	39, 51
London Planetarium	21
London Silver Vaults	37
London Symphony Orchestra (See Barbican Centre)	40, 46
London Toy and Model Museum	19
London Transport Museum	19
London Wall (See also Roman Wall)	38, 51
London Waterbus Company	36
London Zoo	15, 36
Lord Mayor's Show	40
Lower Marsh Market	31
Madame Tussauds	22
Mall Galleries	17
Mansion House	40, 43
Marshall Street Centre	25
Marx Memorial Library	48, 49
Mermaid Theatre	46
Middle Temple Hall	44
Monument	43
Museum in Docklands	52
Museum of Design	57
Museum of Garden History	30

Museum of Instruments	9
Museum of London	41
Museum of Mankind	19
Museum of Methodism	49
National Army Museum	9
National Film Theatre	31
National Gallery	17
National Museum of Labour History	53
National Portrait Gallery	18
National Postal Museum	41
National Sound Archive of the British Library	9
National Theatre	30
National Theatre Company	29
Natural History Museum	10
New Caledonian Market	58
Notting Hill Carnival	7
Oasis Sports Centre	37
Old Bailey (See Central Criminal Court)	41
Old Curiosity Shop	35
Old Vic Theatre	30
Operating Theatre, Old St. Thomas'	57
Paddington Recreation Ground	25
Percival David Foundation Of Chinese Art	34
Petrie Museum of Egyptian Archaeology	35
Petticoat Lane Market	54
Petticoat Lane Designer Fashion Market	54
Photographers' Gallery	34
Place Theatre	33
Pollocks Toy Museum	19
Porchester Centre	25
Portobello Road Market	13
Prince Henry's Room	43
Priory Church of St. Bartholemew the Great	44
Public Records Office	35
Queen Mother's Sports Centre	25
Queen's Gallery	18
Regents Canal	15, 36
Regents Park	25
Riverboat Information Service	5
River and Canal Trips	5
Roman Road Market	54
Roman Wall	38, 43
Roof Gardens	12
Royal Academy of Arts	18
Royal Albert Hall	7, 24
Royal Courts of Justice	21, 39, 40

INDEX

Royal Exchange (See London International Financial Futures Exchange)	44
Royal Festival Hall	30
Royal Fusiliers Museum (See Tower of London)	54
Royal Hospital, Chelsea	8, 11
Royal Mews	22
Royal Mint Development	52
Royal Shakespeare Company (See Barbican Centre)	40, 46
St. Brides	45
St. Catherine's House	22
St. Clement Danes	22
St. Etheldreda's	36
St. Giles Church, Cripplegate	40, 45
St. Giles-in-the-Fields	36
St. James (Clerkenwell)	50
St. James (Piccadilly)	23
St. James's Park	24
St. John's, Smith Square	24
St. Katharine's Dock	51, 55
St. Margaret's	23
St. Martin-in-the-Fields	23
St. Pancras Old Church	36
St. Peter's Italian Church	48, 50
St. Paul's Cathedral	39, 45
Saatchi Collection	18
Sadlers Wells Theatre	28, 47, 50
Samuel Pepys Exhibition (See Prince Henry's Room)	43
Sanctuary (Ladies only)	25
Science Museum	10
Sedgwick Sports Centre	53
Serpentine Gallery	18
Shakespeare Globe Museum	57
Sir John Soane's Museum	35
Smithfield Market	46
Society of Genealogists	49
Somers Town Cycle Route	37
South Bank Complex	30
South Bank Concert Halls	30
South Bank Crafts Centre	31
Southwark Cathedral	56, 58
Spitalfields (Brady) Centre	53
Spitalfields Market	46
Staple Inn	36
State Opening of Parliament	16
Stock Exchange	38, 44
Tate Gallery	18
Telecom Technology Showcase	41
Temple	43
Temple Bar	44
Temple Church	46
Temple of Mithras	43
Theatre Museum	20
Theatres – See list (See also Bloomsbury Theatre)	26-28
Thomas Coram Foundation for Children	34
Tobacco Dock	52
Tower Bridge	55
Tower of London	54
Travelcard	4
Trocadero Centre	16
Trooping the Colour Ceremony	16
Victoria and Albert Museum	10
Vintners' Hall	42
Wallace Collection	18
Wapping Centre	53
Wellcome Museum of the History of Medicine (See Science Museum)	10
Wesley's House and Museum of Methodism	49
Westminster Abbey	23
Westminster Cathedral	23
Westbourne Green Sports Complex	25
Whitbread Stables	50
Whitechapel Art Gallery	53
Whitechapel Waste Market	54
Zamana Gallery	9

PUBLICATIONS

OTHER TITLES IN THE SERIES

Exploring Outer London £2.25
An introduction to lesser known attractions and activities in London's Boroughs.

* Traditional London £1.80
An introduction to London's major traditions — events, places and people.

Children's London £1.65
To help plan family visits. Lists attractions and activities for children of all ages.

* London Made Easy £1.80
London's attractions and facilities for the older visitor and the disabled.

* Available Spring 1987.

MORE UNUSUAL BOOKS

A Capital Guide For Kids £2.30
(Allison & Bushby)
A helpful guide for parents with pre-school age children.

Cheap Eating in London £3.95
(Orbis)
A fun guide for eating out in London for under £6!

A Child's History of London £3.35
(B.B.C.)
A lavishly illustrated history of London.

Ghosts of London
(Jarrold Colour Publications)
East End, City and North £2.75
West End, South and West £2.75

London's Rock Landmarks £5.95
(Omnibus Press)
The A-Z Guide to London's Rock Geography.

Rhyming Cockney Slang £1.50
(Abson Books)
A glossary of Cockney slang which won't break "the iron tank"!

USEFUL PUBLICATIONS

Where to Stay in London £2.45
LVCB's guide to accommodation.

Blue Guide to London £10.95
(A. & C. Black)
Detailed guide with historical background and maps.

Green Guide £5.40
(Michelin)
A new edition of the popular sightseeing guide.

A-Z London Map £1.60
Large scale pocket map of central London with street index.

Coloured A-Z £2.95
New improved version of ever popular street atlas.

London Guide £2.60
(Nicholsons)
Famous guide to Londons sights and services.

**A Time Out Guide
Shopping in London** £3.90
The insiders guide to over 2,000 best value, unusual and specialist shops.

**A Time Out Guide
Eating Out in London** £3.90
Over 1,350 of the best dining, drinking and lunching places in town.

A Capital Companion £15.00
(Webb & Bower)

HOW TO ORDER

Publications can be ordered from Sales Department, LVCB 26 Grosvenor Gardens, London SW1W 0DU. Prices include postage and packing.

A wide selection of books on London can be found at the LVCB Bookshop, Tourist Information Centre, Victoria Station, SW1.

Prices quoted are for 1986 and are subject to change.